SKETCH OF RAILWAY NETWORK OF

METRO-LAND

A GLORIOUS UNSPOILED COUNTRYSIDE, SITUATED IN MIDDLESEX, HERTS AND BUCKS, EASILY AND QUICKLY REACHED BY THE METROPOLITAN RAILWAY

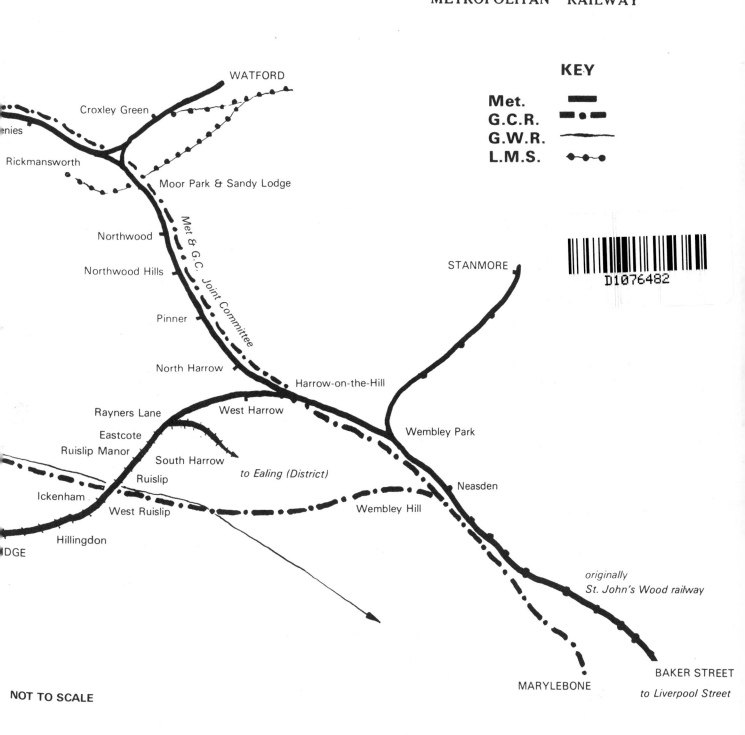

KEY

Met.	━━
G.C.R.	━ ∙ ━
G.W.R.	───
L.M.S.	●─●─●

ton

WATFORD

Croxley Green

nies

Rickmansworth

Moor Park & Sandy Lodge

Met & G.C. Joint Committee

Northwood

Northwood Hills

STANMORE

Pinner

North Harrow

Harrow-on-the-Hill

Rayners Lane   West Harrow

Eastcote

Wembley Park

Ruislip Manor

South Harrow

to Ealing (District)

Ruislip

Ickenham

Neasden

West Ruislip

Wembley Hill

Hillingdon

DGE

originally
St. John's Wood railway

BAKER STREET

MARYLEBONE

to Liverpool Street

NOT TO SCALE

The Romance of Metro-Land

Metro-land beckoned us out to lanes in beechy Bucks —
Goldschmidt and Howland (in a wooden hut beside the station)
'Most attractive sites
Ripe for development'; Charrington's for coal;
And not far off the neo-Tudor shops.

Sir John Betjeman 'Summoned by Bells'

The Romance of Metro-Land

A further armchair odyssey through the countryside
served by the old Metropolitan Railway.

DENNIS EDWARDS & RON PIGRAM

BLOOMSBURY BOOKS

London

By the same authors
Metro Memories
The Golden Years of the Metropolitan Railway
The Final Link

First published in 1979 by Midas Books

Reprinted 1983

Reprinted 1986 by
BATON TRANSPORT
1 Russell Chambers
London, WC2E 8AA

© Dennis F. Edwards and
Ron Pigram, 1979

This edition published 1988 by
Bloomsbury Books an imprint of
Godfrey Cave Associates Limited
42 Bloomsbury Street, London
WC1B 3QJ under license from Baton
Transport/Cleveland Press

ISBN 1 870630 37 8

Printed in Yugoslavia

The Authors

Ron Pigram has been involved
with history and the countryside
all his professional life. He admits
(with reluctance) that his interest
with the Metropolitan Railway
stretches back to the last days of
the old Company when his father
was invited to manage the Brill
Branch, deep in the Vale of
Aylesbury.

He has remained an adopted
countryman, treading the
footpaths of the Chiltern Hills
through which the Met ran. His
first book on the area appeared in
1970, and later works have
included *Metro Memories* — the
sister volume to this book, and
Around the Historic Chilterns in
the Midas History of the English
Countryside series.

He is a Member of the
Chartered Institute of Transport
and has lectured on the history of
'Metro-land' and the topography
of the region. He is also a founder
member and Press Officer of the
Hitchin Historical Society.

Dennis F. Edwards was born in a
typical suburban 'semi' in
Metro-land. Now in his 40s,
married with a young daughter, he
lives within sound of the railway
on the Uxbridge Line. He is a
confirmed environmentologist,
and is Publicity Officer for a local
Civic Trust Group. He has also
written a number of local history
and walks books.

Frontispiece:
**'Just a moment while I look at the
map'** . . . Walkers in the 1920s
pausing outside Amersham's Town
Hall having travelled by Met train
and completed the walk down the
valley through Rectory Wood. The
girls wear chamberpot hats, and one
of the men is completely dressed
with Trilby hat and plus-fours.
Walkers in pre-war days were prepared to tackle very long walks by
modern standards, many books
suggested tours of over 15 miles.
Authors' Collection

Acknowledgements

The authors must thank the many
people whose deep love and interest
in *Metro-land* since the appearance
of our first book have encouraged
us again, especially private
photographers who are mentioned
in the following pages. The County
Museum Authorities at Aylesbury
and Leicester; and the local Library
curators at Uxbridge, Wembley,
Watford and elsewhere have
answered so generously our calls for
professional help and use of their
archives.

Front Cover Illustration: Metropolitan Railway electrification; an artist's
impression of the newly extended electric train service to Rickmansworth in 1925,
showing Metropolitan-Vickers electric locomotive No. 17 'Florence Nightingale'.

Contents

To: M. & P.

'Metro-land is a country with elastic boundaries which each visitor can draw for himself as Stevenson drew his map of *Treasure Island.* It lies mainly in Bucks; but choice fragments of Middlesex and Hertfordshire may be annexed at pleasure. As much of the countryside as you can comfortably cover on foot from one Metropolitan Railway station to another you may add to your private and individual map of Metro-land.'

'Metro-land is a country of hills and valleys, ridges and hollows, with a few broad plateaus. Go where you will, the landscape is well farmed; the eye ranges from wood to wood, from tower to steeple. And there is good tillage as well as whin-clad common, and fields which still laugh with golden corn.'

   'This is a good parcel of English soil in which to build a home and take root . . . the new settlement of Metro-land proceeds apace; the new colonists thrive again.'

'If you are seeking a home — large or small, old world or modern, you will readily find it in Metro-land — the glorious countryside easily and quickly reached by the Metropolitan Railway. The train service is frequent; the season ticket rates are low; the Educational facilities are excellent and the local golf courses both numerous and good.'

                                                              Metropolitan Railway literature

Introduction

METROPOLITAN RAILWAY

The Message of Metro-land

About the time of the First World War, the word Metro-land was just an advertising idea. It was the basic theme of a campaign launched by the old Metropolitan Railway Company, which had started steam Underground railways in London and which aspired to be one of England's great main-line companies.

Later in the 20s and 30s, as people strove for a better, cleaner existence after the 'war to end all wars', Metro-land came to mean much more. It did not refer merely to the countryside outside London near the Chiltern Hills, through which the railway was busily promoting its new houses, but a vision of what life could hold. It conjured up visions of a suburban paradise within reach of green fields and woods, quiet well-ordered avenues of houses with indoor sanitation and perhaps a hint of coloured glass in the doors, as well as room for gardens in which sturdy children could play happily amid the flowers and coloured decorative gnomes eternally squatting near ornamental ponds.

For others, who were unable to free themselves from the dirt and drab browns of the London streets, the railway promoted its Metro-land as the friendly green playground for walkers and cyclists.

But far away from London, these Metro-land promotions were overlaid on the timelessness of a country society where the patterns

The Father of Metro-land

Sir Edward Watkin, who transformed a struggling company to a forceful expansionist railway, with his vision of the Metropolitan as a main-line company that would have linked the Midlands with the Channel Ports.

Authors' Collection

of nature were destined to outlive the railway itself. It is this odd mix of events that will always make Metro-land a special place — a slightly dotty world so peculiarly English, where Pullman car expresses could run every day past the new mass estates to a tiny country station miles from any big town, and where once-proud steam locomotives that had hauled trains beneath Westminster could be found, topped by the odd farmyard fowl, in a forgotten spot innocent of any noise, in the heart of England somewhere near Oxford.

But as has been explained, the purpose of the Metropolitan Railway had, for most of the Victorian age, been confined to running Underground services in the capital. This book takes a look at the recent past; to do so we should first see why London needed a subterranean railway and then examine the way in which the Metropolitan Railway exploited the advantages of electric haulage over steam locomotion, gradually pushing the age of steam back into the countryside itself, where it lingered for many years.

The Pioneer Line
The Metropolitan Railway, which first ran in 1863, was part of the development of Victorian London. As in its later days, it was essentially involved with the expansion of new housing estates.

The Met's Last Chairman
Sir Charles McLaren, Bart, KC, MP, who became Chairman of the Metropolitan Railway in 1904, took over during a period of changing fortunes when the electrification of the railway was well under way. In 1902 he received a Baronetcy, became a Privy Councillor in 1908, and three years later became Lord Aberconway of Bodnant.

Authors' Collection

The Crystal Way

One of the early proposals for an underground railway in London which was considered by the Select Committee on Metropolitan Communications, published in July 1855. Clearly derived from the successful Crystal Palace of 1851, the plan was devised by Sir Joseph Paxton as a 'Grand Circle Railway' and, with its boulevard above the tracks, was considered by contemporary critics to present features of 'remarkable novelty'. Other schemes were put forward by eminent railway engineers of the age, including Stephenson, Locke and Page.

Authors' Collection

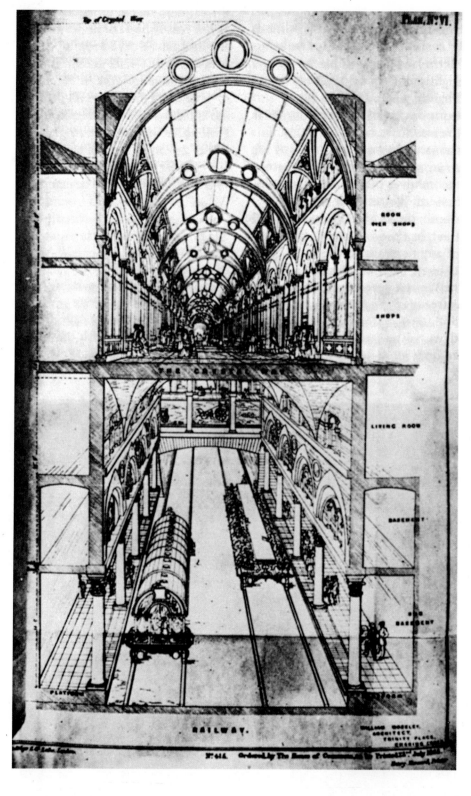

Before the first Metropolitan trains ran, the Ladbroke and Notting Hill estates under developers of the day such as Cubitt, and the Paddington estates of the Bishop of London, had already been started. Even as far as St John's Wood there was building activity: Thomas Hood wrote in one of his very last poems before he died in 1842:

*'Where are ye, London's meads
  and bowers
And gardens redolent of flowers,
Wherein the zephyr wons?
Alas! Moorfields are fields no
  more!
See Hatton's garden builded all
  o'er;
And that bare wood — St
  John's.'*

Building under London
The dual tracking for standard and wide gauge trains has been completed. The massive timber roof shoring is still in place on the right-hand tunnel.

Authors' Collection

The Western Extension
A street scene at Paddington in 1868, after the extension from Edgware Road to Gloucester Road had opened on 1 October.

Authors' Collection

From 1811 until 1853 the number of dwelling houses in the City of London had actually fallen by 155 yet the 'sleeping population', estimated at 120,000, had increased by about 4000. There was an overflow and thousands walked many miles to their work in the City. Before the railway, the pedestrians were joined by hundreds of carts, primitive omnibuses, coach-and-fours owned by wealthy merchants, and cockney traders aside their cobs.

The Great Western Railway, which had been unable to build its terminus closer to the centre than Paddington, was naturally anxious to carry its passengers all the way into the City. The Board found itself sympathetic to the wishes of the City fathers who looked for a new railway link with the expanding western suburbs. There were a number of fanciful ideas, including a subterranean Crystal Way. But in the end it was largely due to Charles Pearson, Solicitor to the Corporation of London, that the successful scheme which became the nucleus of the Metropolitan Railway got off the ground.

Pearson gave freely both of his enthusiasm and his money. 'I remember Mr Pearson telling me he had spent £8000 out of his own pocket in placing a Metropolitan railway service before the public', Lord Mayor McArthur said in 1881.

Finally, Pearson persuaded the Corporation to find £200,000 to add to the £175,000 already put up by the Great Western Railway in order to build an underground railway. Ten years were to pass

11

'Yesterday Mary Anne and I made our first trip down the "drain". We walked to the Edgware Road and took First Class for King's Cross (6d each). We experienced no disagreeable odour, beyond the smell common to tunnels. The carriages hold ten persons, with divided seats, and are lighted by gas (two lights). They are also so lofty that a six-footer may stand erect with his hat on. Trains run every 15 minutes from six in the morning till twelve at night (with some slight variations) and about 30,000 are conveyed on the line daily; shares have risen, and there is a prospect of a large dividend.'

William Hardman 'A Mid-Victorian Pepys' 26 January 1863

Mind the Doors! A cry perhaps first heard on 10 January 1863, as the first public train on the Metropolitan Railway leaves Bishop's Road, Paddington. This illustration, from the *Illustrated London News,* shows the popularity of the early trains.

It could be highly dangerous to stand close to early locomotives. On 9 May, 1864, one of the boilers burst just as a train was leaving this station. A witness wrote 'The enginemen had narrow escapes, and an omnibus in the Harrow Road, 200 yards away was nearly hit by the dome of the boiler which had been sent heavenwards like a skyrocket'. In the train opposite, R. H. Burnett, the Locomotive Superintendent, had lowered his window to see the machine leave. He was only 16 feet away when the top plates went up, and he thought that the 'end of the world had come'.

Authors' Collection

before the work was finished.

The pioneer railway proved very popular and the crush at Paddington on the first day was as great 'as at the doors of a theatre on the first night of some popular performance'. But there was trouble, not long after, with the Great Western Railway which had provided the original locomotives and carriages. The Metropolitan Company was able to borrow rolling stock and some hastily-converted locomotives from the Great Northern Railway, whose passengers were soon able to travel over a junction at its King's Cross terminus to reach the Metropolitan's Farringdon terminus direct. This event was toasted with such elation that the Farringdon buffet ran out of liquor almost at once. Almost 10 million passengers were carried by the railway in the first year, 1863.

Steam under London

Fowler, the first Engineer of the Metropolitan, had planned to use locomotives carrying stored steam, but care had been taken when constructing the underground railway to leave ventilation space to enable steam from the locomotives to escape. The Select Committee of the House of Lords had been told, in 1853, that railway signals in the tunnels would be so obscured by steam and smoke as to be invisible. Immediately the line opened, alarmist paragraphs appeared in the daily papers headed 'Choke Damp'. To allay public panic, a small fan and an engine were arranged to blow fresh air into Portland Road station, and side glasses were removed from Gower Street Station. The early stations had great glass and timber roofs which did not extend to the full length of the platforms. Again, this was done to allow steam to escape.

However, in spite of condensing apparatus fitted to the locomotives using the line that was eventually to become the Inner Circle, the atmosphere and tunnel ventilation of the

Met proved a constant source of trouble until the introduction of electric power.

During the days of steam on the underground lines of the Metropolitan Railway, coaling was carried out at certain stations, including Baker Street, and Farringdon, by means of one hundredweight wicket baskets which were stacked on the platforms near the stationary position of the engines. The stacks were under the charge of a coalman.

It was the fireman's duty to help the coalman lift the basket and empty it into the engine bunker. The amount was recorded against the driver for his bonus — the Metropolitan's coal consumption bonus considered only mileage (it was exactly 12 miles and 70 chains around the Inner Circle) and the coal consumed. The lower the coal consumption per mile, the larger the bonus paid to the driver. In the Metropolitan's original offices in Westbourne Terrace, Paddington, it could be noted that certain drivers were experts in coal economy, and had their names high on the bonus lists.

It was inevitable that the underground steam railways were smoke-ridden and unhealthy places. It is doubtful, however, whether there is any truth in the story that the engineers wore long beards as primitive filters! The Victorian male favoured hair on the face, but the smuts pervaded everything. First experiences of travelling in the steam-hauled underground carriages was terrifying. Between stations, passengers inhaled a noxious mixture of steam, coal smoke, soot and sulphur. Jets of dirt puffed through every small hole around the doors and windows, as one Met traveller remembered. The public did not complain, but many paused at their destination, inhaling deeply from the less contaminated air near the station exits.

One case which was discussed at the turn of the century illustrated the travelling conditions that Driver Turner (page 119) and his colleagues

Portland Road Station:—European View

This was how a German artist saw the new wonder of London — the Metropolitan Railway under the Marylebone Road at what was later Great Portland Street Station. Above are the crowded streets full of traffic jams. Below the frequent, fast trains convey passengers to and from the City. But the artist used a lot of licence — where is the appalling smoke and steam and soot?

Marylebone Library

experienced every day on the Met. A rather old, lame and stout lady was travelling from Aldersgate Street. Because of her infirmity, she was forced to step down from the train backwards, taking great care. The enthusiastic station staff, spotting her in the murk assumed that she was boarding and that she had become stuck in the doorway. She was heaved in and 'right away' waved. Incredibly, this accident was repeated later, despite her choking pleas (addressed to the interior of the carriage). She was almost asphyxiated by the pungent railway fumes and when her plight was finally revealed she had to be rushed to St Mary's Hospital, Paddington.

The shareholders of the Company were conscious of the problem of smoke. In 1881 Dr Turle suggested that something

should be done to ensure better ventilation between Edgware Road and King's Cross. A number of voices supported him, saying that if it were a coal mine, large fans would be the answer. The Chairman of the Met, however, at this time had his eyes firmly on the approval of a sum of £370,000 for his extension to Aylesbury, on which he had set his heart.

The railway lamp of the early railway age added an element of gloom to the carriages once a train was out of range of the station lights. The lamp consisted of a thick glass vessel, fixed to the roof of a carriage, filled with animal oil, and in which hung a wick. To light this equipment called for experience and determination: even when the light was burning, it was fitful and fought for existence in a nauseous odou.. The Metropolitan

decided to illuminate its carriages with gas. Compressed gas cylinders were unknown, so it was carried in collapsible india rubber bags hung outside the carriages and connected to the jets inside. For the first time, people could read on a train with the aid of artificial light. Later, the Metropolitan had its own gas-manufacturing plant at its new works at Neasden.

Ventilation shafts from the tunnels to the roads above can still be seen. They were a practical solution which was made possible by road rebuilding, but they also provided amusement for the Marylebone street urchins. Newly-arrived visitors from the country had no idea what created the huge clouds of steam that often arose from the gratings. In an age when it was indecent to expose the ankles, many an embarrassed young Edwardian miss found her light summer dress billowing around her shoulders — much to the appreciation of local male Londoners!

Developments, Wrangles and Watkin

The Metropolitan Railway grew quickly, westwards at first, as a separate company, to Hammersmith, an area then still filled with orchards where early strawberries and soft fruit were urged to early harvest for London tables. This extension was opened in June 1864 and a branch built to Hammersmith Road (later Addison Road and Olympia). Next came the extension eastwards to Moorgate Street (where the company was later to consider the erection of a hotel). The first section of the St John's Wood Railway — what was later to become the main line to Metroland — was opened in 1868. It was an age of expansion.

Here it is necessary to introduce the Metropolitan's early hero — Sir Edward Watkin (1910-1901) — the *enfant terrible* of the Victorian railway world. It was under his direction that the Metropolitan Railway broke out of London into the countryside in an attempt to become a great main-line railway company. Watkin's personality clashed with that of James Staat Forbes, Chairman of the District Railway. This had been formed to create the southern part of the Underground railway that would eventually complete the Inner Circle.

It is outside the scope of this account to trace the difficulties except to state that Watkin dismissed the proposals of Forbes for an Inner Circle Completion Company, which he described as 'a bogus company, whose directors have repudiated every personal liability, with no shareholders and no money'. Forbes replied, with heavy sarcasm that 'The Metropolitan are important people, presided over by a great genius'. It was only by outside intervention

Bound for Hammersmith

The crew of Beyer Peacock locomotive No. 55, exposed to the open air, seem glad to be running tender foremost, with steam up. This engine was one of the second type of condensing engines built by Beyer and was delivered in 1880, and was sold for scrap in 1906, when the London lines had been electrified.

The Metropolitan's brick red livery and large yellow numbers had been introduced by J. J. Hanbury, Locomotive Superintendent in 1885, who had come from the Midland Railway.

Note the unsafe position of an employee standing below the platform. The locomotive was designed to carry cold water in special tanks for steam condensing purposes, the cylinders being placed outside to make way for them.

For many years, the resulting hot water was discharged on the completion of every journey — either at Farringdon or Moorgate, and replaced by cold. The tunnels were generally fresher when this was done. When trains ran round the Inner Circle, this cleansing of water was found irksome, and only fresh water for boiler requirements was taken on. The water was often warm before use, and so ineffective for condensing. The foulness of the tunnels in later steam days was quite avoidable, but the Metropolitan and the District Railways found it was cheaper to defy public opinion than trouble with the earlier precautions.

London Transport

that the two companies were persuaded to work together in order to complete the important link in 1894.

Sir Edward Watkin had become Chairman of the Metropolitan in 1872 at a time when the Company's accounts were in a mess: John Parson (who seems to have been the person responsible) frankly told a committee of enquiry that he 'did not understand the figures'.

Watkin was a walking encyclopedia of railway knowledge and experience. Starting his career in a goods office of the London and North Western Railway, he became Chairman of the South Eastern Railway and of the Manchester, Sheffield and Lincolnshire Railway. He was to be the Metropolitan's Chairman for twenty-two years. It was under Watkin that the Metropolitan began its expansion into the countryside of Middlesex, Buckinghamshire and Hertfordshire to realise its self-appointed destiny as a great trunk railway, linking the Manchester, Sheffield & Lincolnshire Railway with the South Eastern Railway and the Channel Tunnel. Watkin put his case to Parliament: 'If the line is made it will make the Metropolitan and South Eastern parts of a system running right through the country — a sort of backbone for the commerce and industry of the country.'

The real intentions of Sir Edward Watkin will possibly never be known as he was a man who kept little correspondence. Certainly, he did dream of linking the Manchester, Sheffield and Lincolnshire Railway to the South Eastern Railway but he also wanted a greater Metropolitan Railway and it was the failure of the Metropolitan to get its proposed link to Worcester in the 1880s that turned all his energies to the 'great link' from Manchester to Dover, via London.

The project for a line to Aylesbury from London was by no means new. There had been many plans from about 1845 onwards,

most of then branched from the London and North Western Railway at or near Wembley.

The Metropolitan line to the Chilterns was for many years known as the 'Extension Line'. It sprang from the single-track Baker Street and St John's Wood line of 1868, and was pushed out into rural Middlesex and beyond in stages. The first extension ran from Swiss Cottage to West Hampstead and the single-track line from Baker Street was doubled. The extension opened on 30 June 1879. The building of the bridges across the valley at Kilburn was not completed until a few months later: the rails reached Willesden on 24 November 1879.

'Amongst the charms of Kilburn is its proximity to the country. Within half an hour's walk the pedestrian is among trees and fields and pleasant places', said a contemporary account.

In 1880 the line reached Harrow, where already houses were spreading out north of the old Hill towards the London and North Western Railway at Wealdstone and Harrow Weald. Here, only a few years before, the lands had been noted for high yields of wheat and bean crops.

'The whole neighbourhood is still more rural than any part of the country within the same distance from the interminable brick and mortar wilderness of London. The district about Kingsbury and Neasden is intersected by green lanes and field paths bordered by flowering hawthorn hedges, while the River Brent meanders through them', ran another account.

From Harrow the new line pushed on to Pinner (1885), Rickmansworth (1887) and Chesham (1889), with a short section to Chalfont.

'The extension of the Metropolitan Railway from London to Pinner, Northwood and Chesham, has opened up a new and delightful countryside to the advantage of picturesque seekers; ancient houses and old-world ways. Within 50

Baker Street: The Birth of Metroland

Building the line to St John's Wood. This scene of 1867 by an artist from the *Illustrated London News* captures the busy site at Baker Street. The navvies of Messrs Lucas and Aird are digging deep down behind what, until recently, were the gardens and houses of Marylebone Road.

The St John's Wood Railway was single track except at stations. The original intention was for the line to go to Hampstead, but it went no further than Swiss Cottage.

The branch opened on Easter Monday 13 April 1868, having been passed by Captain Taylor of the Board of Trade the previous Saturday. There was an official tour of the branch on 18 April and the usual celebration lunch, which took place at Marlborough Road Station.

'The railway is constructed as a single line at present, with double lines at stations. Provision is made for a double line and extension to Hampstead. The capacity of the line is expected to be 60,000 persons daily', said the *London Illustrated News* report.

Marylebone Library

Steam Power

Beyer Peacock locomotive No. 49 approaches Aldgate Station. A locomotive working the New Cross service takes on coal and water on the left. The date of this picture is about 1904, not long before the lines were due to be electrified and a new era commenced. Number 49 was built in 1870 and re-boilered in the early 1890s. She was one of the last survivors of her class and was scrapped as late as 1936.

London Transport

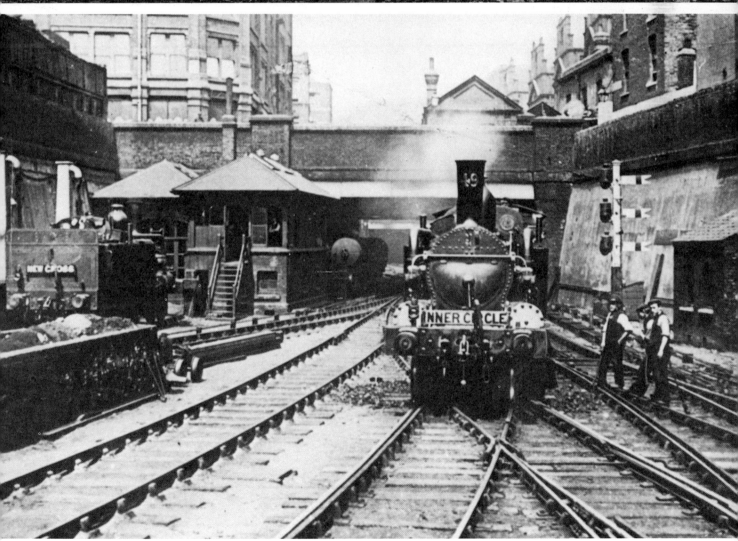

minutes from Baker Street and for the cost of less than a florin (10p.), if the visitor be economically disposed, he can enjoy a feast of good things, fresh air, noble parks, stately houses, magnificent trees and sylvan streams,' it rhapsodised.

The new line through Rickmansworth was inspected by Major-General Hutchinson of the Board of Transport on 30 August 1887 and the train services started on 1 September. A month later, the *Watford Observer* said that as many as 450 people had alighted at Harrow the previous Sunday and 250 people at Northwood.

But not everybody thought the new line was a good idea and a reader of the *Financial News* complained that 'so boring was the country passed through and so few people on the train' that he considered that the extension 'was a waste of money and doomed to failure'.

In 1891, the Metropolitan Railway purchased the Aylesbury and Buckingham Railway and the Extension line was constructed from Chalfont through Amersham and Wendover to a point just outside Aylesbury (1892). In 1899 the Manchester, Sheffield & Lincolnshire Railway finally reached Aylesbury (linking with the Metropolitan's Aylesbury and Buckingham Railway at Quainton Road) and Manchester trains began running through to the new terminus of what was now the Great Central Railway at Marylebone. On 2 April 1902, the Extension Line from Harrow to Quainton Road was administered by a new body, the Metropolitan and Great Central Joint Committee.

Into the Metro-land Age
To return to the days of Watkin: Despite commercial distress in the early 1880s, when Watkin claimed that the first class passenger was travelling second and the second

The Met Expands

Among improvements to the Metropolitan's inner London system in the early 1920s was the linking up and utilisation of an old length of tunnel that ran parallel with the Metropolitan near St Pancras station so as to allow Met trains to switch over to the 'Widened Lines' and so have an alternative route to Moorgate. The old tunnel built in the 1860s was about 1200 feet in length. The work, according to the Met's publicity of the time 'will have a far-reaching effect of doubling the most important section of the Inner Circle, enabling the Company's increasingly popular through Metroland-City trains to be expedited in both directions'.

Authors' Collection

By Metropolitan through Regent Street

The Metropolitan horse bus services started in August 1866 and ended in September 1901. The company supplied buses and fare-taking facilities, and the contractor (the chief contractor was Crews) found the horses and the drivers. This three-horse bus was painted yellow and seated six first class, and eleven second class and third class passengers inside, with seven first class, seventeen second and third class outside. There were four seats beside the driver — always a popular position. A purple umbrella bearing the words 'Metropolitan Railway' helped shelter the driver and advertise the bus. This photograph, kindly supplied by Mr Charles Lee, was exhibited in Lord Aberconway's office at Baker Street until the very last day of the Metropolitan Railway in 1933.

Charles E. Lee

Off to the Gaiety
One of the many contractors who hurried Met passengers from London stations to the theatre seventy years ago. An advertisement from the 1904 Met guide.

Authors' Collection

class third, the railway expanded. Maintenance facilities were increasingly strained at the old Chapel Street works at Edgware Road and at Farringdon, where there was a carriage shed on the south side of the line and a turntable on the other. Watkin told shareholders in 1881 that this land was cramped for workshops and expensive 'because you ought not to have workshops on land that might sell for large sums per foot'.

He told them about the cheap land at Neasden where there was a level surface and 'country air for the people you employ, and we shall be able to do our work there more rapidly'. So the Neasden Works was born, and by 1882 contracts were placed for the repair shops and workmen's cottages. The streets were at first just identified by letters (e.g. 'A' Street). Later they received names associated with Metropolitan places — hence

Verney Street and others. The
houses were let for 'moderate
rentals'.

When the Great Central Railway
way reached London there was a
proposal that the Neasden works
should be transferred to the new
company, and a fresh site found for
the Metropolitan out at Stoke
Mandeville. The two companies,
however, had decided to go their
separate ways some years earlier,
when the Great Central Railway's
Marylebone terminus was built. The
Metropolitan spent over £97,000
on electrical equipment in the early
1900s, and the last of the steam
locomotives were withdrawn from
the lines south of Finchley Road

The Great Exhibitions
The Metropolitan was aware, at a
very early stage, of the revenue to
be gained from activities other than
the carriage of passengers. The
formation of the Metropolitan
Railway Estate Company is told
later in these pages. It was Watkin
who pointed out in the early years
that only 4½% of receipts came
from goods traffic, while other
railways obtained 50%. The profits

from the carriage of goods, minerals
and parcels continued to be less
than those forecast. In 1904 they
were £187,891 and fell dramati-
cally, after the Great Central Railway route opened two years later,
to little more than £70,000.

In the 1860s the railway was
responsible for the huge basement
under Smithfield Meat Market, then
the 'largest example of wrought
iron girder and brick arch construction in existence'. Hydraulic lifts
conveyed the goods from the basement to the stores.

Later Met enterprises were
Watkin's Tower at Wembley,
designed to rival the Eiffel Tower
and to be a source of extra
passenger traffic. It was a failure,
but barely had its scrap metal been
exported to Italy, when the great
Franco-British Exhibition opened
at White City in 1908. This gave
rise to hopes for improved
passenger traffic. The 1909 Show,
however, was a failure and the
number of passengers carried to
White City on the Hammersmith
branch fell away. Dividends
were maintained by an improve-
ment in goods and parcels services.
In 1910 came the Japan-British
Exhibition and the railway stressed

Bluejackets to the Rescue

The scene at Farringdon on 6 May 1915, following a severe thunderstorm. The tracks were flooded to a depth of two feet near the old Ray Street 'Grid Iron' bridge. Two horse-drawn fire engines were placed on wagons, and naval personnel assisted the Met's engineering staff with pumping the water away. On the right is locomotive No. 26, which was fitted with a steam pump on the front buffer.

London Transport

the convenience of its frequent services to the grounds.

At the exhibition large ornamental lakes, fountains and funfairs added to the fascination of the goods from the East. In fact, the White City continued its rôle as a pleasure centre until the First World War, when the buildings were used for armament work.

After the war, during which more than a third of the Metropolitan employees left for the Front or were engaged on war work, preparations were begun for the greatest exhibition of all — the British Empire Exhibition of 1924-25 at Wembley Park, where the Tower had once stood.

Wembley traffic broke all records: 740 Metropolitan trains

left Baker Street in an almost unbroken line every day. Some 107,250 trains were run to Wembley during the first season, carrying 11,500,000 passengers.

There was, indeed, excitement in the air: the Metropolitan Railway wooed its passengers in the 1920s and 1930s with advertisements: 'for natural beauty, ease of access and healthfulness, no district around London can surpass the claims of Metro-land. Its train service is frequent . . . its season ticket rates are low.' The slogan used in all publicity was 'Live in Metro-land': this included the series of delightful guide-books which the railway published from 1915 onwards called *Metro-land.* The slogan even appeared engraved on the door

plates of the trains themselves.

New lines were opened to Watford (1925) and Stanmore (1932) and electrification extended to Rickmansworth.

The Rise of Metro-Land

The north-western suburbs of London were largely a creation of the Metropolitan Railway. Places such as Dollis Hill, Preston Road, Kingsbury and Rayners Lane either did not exist, or were tiny hamlets, before the railway was built. The Metropolitan Railway was unique in that it had legal powers to grant building leases and to sell ground rents — a privilege which had come about as a result of legal battles during the early days of the Metro-

politan in the City. It was in order to tidy up the mess that the Metropolitan Surplus Lands Committee was formed under the Metropolitan Railway Acts of 1885 and 1887. It was sometime afterwards, however, that somebody in the Metropolitan offices said: 'Why not use some of the land we have out in the country for building houses? The people who buy the houses could then travel to town on our trains — and increase the revenues.' The Committee agreed, and the very first estate was built alongside Pinner station at Cecil Park. 'Unique and tasteful, thoroughly well-built houses and also plots of land for sale for the erection of houses of good class', said the first advertisements. The principles of home ownership were

Neasden: Homes for the Workers

The Metropolitan always looked after the welfare of its men and when the works opened at Neasden, a small village was laid out near the banks of the River Brent. Later, the streets of the railway settlement were named after places on the far-flung ends of the system: Verney Street, Brill Street, etc.

London Borough of Brent

Cattle Wagon and Brake Van

The Metropolitan relied heavily on its goods and parcel traffic from the rural parts of Metro-land. In 1904, for example, goods traffic amounted to £152,898 compared with passenger traffic receipts of £643,330.

Authors' Collection

Metro-land for a Penny
Funny old cottages, rose-red
ancient bricks that seem to grow
drowsy in the soft afternoon
sun . . . in Metro-land time could
stand still and there was only the
scent of flowers and the noise of
drowsy bees. These Metro-land
guides were issued each year and
were remarkable for the carefully
coloured plates they contained
(inside as well as the cover) in an
age before the dawn of colour
photography.

Authors' Collection

METRO-LAND
PRICE ONE PENNY

set out in the Committee's estate
prospectus: 'The many advantages
of ownership must be obvious to
every household. A tenant has
the uneasy feeling that the lease
is running out and that he may
receive notice to quit. The owner-
occupier has the gratification of
knowing that so long as the
property belongs to him, all the
improvements he may make to the
house and garden are for his own
benefit and that of his family — not
for the landlord.'

However, Cecil Park was not the
first building estate in Metro-land.

Within a few weeks of the line
opening through Northwood, the
Eastbury Estate had been sold for
building and the *Watford Observer*
said that 53 plots had been sold
near the station: 'A rare opportunity for small capitalists and
speculators.' The town began to
develop into a pleasant upper
middle-class district. 'Yet only a
few minutes away is a charming
landscape . . . tiny hills and
hollows . . . pools of water,
brambly wildernesses, where in
spring nightingales sing and the air
is sweet with the scent of violets,

Architect, C. W. Clark.

RESIDENCE ON CEDAR'S ESTATE, RICKMANSWORTH.

Metro-land Arcadia
The Metropolitan Railway Country Estates, a limited company formed by the Met in 1919, busily enchanted the middle-classes with a prospect of fine homes in quiet unspoilt countryside — so forming the romantic image of Metro-land. Rows of uncrowded well-designed houses could be bought, with a wide choice of stained glass front door panels depicting bluebirds in flight, stately galleons, or the broad orange rays of sun (a great favourite, this) that were refracted in myriad flecks of coloured light through the hallways (usually painted with a decent brown varnish). Arcadia, indeed, with rates around 50p!

Authors' Collection

HOUSING DEVELOPMENT IN METRO-LAND.

IN view of the Estate developments which have taken place in Metro-land and the additional facilities which are now being provided by the extension of the electrified line from Harrow to Rickmansworth, it will not be out of place to give some indication of the active housing development that is taking place in Metro-land.

The Metropolitan Railway Company has, principally by the excellent train service between Metro-land and Baker Street, and the City, and through its affiliated Land Companies been able to develop several large Estates on those portions of the land nearest to town, and on these have been built, amid charming surroundings, a large number of houses which combine beauty with utility.

The principal Estate now being developed is the Cedars Estate, 500 acres in extent, which is notable for its delightful situation and for its abundance of charming features, and no more delectable spot could be desired as a place of residence. It is undulating in character; possesses a subsoil of gravel, sand and chalk; is conveniently situated near Rickmansworth Station, and extends from this old-world country town westward over hill, dale and broad woodland to Chorley Wood's breezy common, where it is flanked by trim plantations that provide a perpetual feast for the eye.

primroses and hawthorn, and in autumn the district is rich with crimson and gold leaves and hedges. This is the haunt of the nightingale. Let us hope that the delighted visitor will listen and let 'em alone.'

With the opening of the Harrow and Uxbridge Railway in 1904, there was some development at Ruislip, where King's College, Cambridge, the principal landowners, released an area off High Street at King's End for the building of high-class housing.

There was also an estate at St Catherine's Manor, along Bury Street at Ruislip. The Ruislip-Northwood Council were the first local authority in England to produce a town plan. There were grand ideas for a garden city on Welwyn and Hampstead Garden City lines, but the First World War put an end to this project.

At Eastcote a few houses were built, whilst out at Rickmansworth and Chorley Wood settlements began of early commuters, including the famous architect, C. F. A. Voysey. His house at Chorley Wood became the prototype for many fine detached and semi-

A DAY IN THE COUNTRY

METROPOLITAN RAILWAY

LONDON'S PLEASURELAND

CHEAP FARE & PLEASURE PARTY
ARRANGEMENTS ON THE METRO.

detached country houses.

But the man who really put Metro-land housing on the map was Robert H. Selbie. He was Secretary of the Metropolitan Railway and in a memo to the Board in 1912 he said that the countryside of Middlesex was 'daily growing in popularity' as a place in which to live. There was a shortage of houses and of suitable sites, and Selbie thought that the Met should advertise its estates. In 1918 he stressed the fact that men were going to return to a better world and that they needed homes in the country, with gardens and space to breathe.

In January 1919 The Metropolitan Railway Country Estates Limited was formed with a capital of £150,000. Many of the directors were also on the Board of the Metropolitan Railway. Henry Gibson, surveyor to the Surplus Lands Committee, was appointed Estate Agent and the offices were set up at Baker Street. Almost immediately the Cedars Estate was purchased at Rickmansworth and also Chalk Hill, Wembley, with some 10¾ acres of land, forming part of Neasden works, being added.

The new company sought to assure investors that 'Railway companies are to be trusted and are not open to the suspicion that often attaches to the speculative builder and estate developer'.

'It is fortunate for prospective purchasers that the large new residential estates at Neasden, Wembley Park and Chorley Wood are controlled by such an organisation as the Metropolitan Railway Country Estates Limited.'

The Metropolitan Estates, where you could either arrange for your own architect or builder to erect a house, or you could buy a home already completed were as follows:

Kingsbury Garden Village Estate, Neasden and Kingsbury —

Here, the Metropolitan literature told prospective buyers:

'Peace and quiet prevail, and the stretches of country around offer plenty of opportunity for invigorating exercise to those who are inclined to walking and cyling. A model garden village on which a number of semi-detached residences have been erected.'
Chalk Hill, Wembley Park —

'In a picturesque locality within close touch of London, yet in open country.'
Woodcock Dell, Preston and Northwick Park, Harrow Garden Village, Rayners Lane —
This was an important estate because it was the first one which was built with the lower middle-class house owner in mind. A local builder, E. S. Reid (who was once Deputy Engineer to Harrow Council) was employed to build the houses. The estate was very popular and the houses even today are still sold as Met houses. Reid advertised extensively in the Metro-land magazines: 'The estate has the particular advantage of being self-contained and wherever you choose a house on this estate you may rest assured that you will be surrounded by other E. S. Reid houses . . . and you may be sure that you will not have a nasty cheap mass-production house anywhere near you to lower the value of your property.'

The other Metropolitan estates on the line to Uxbridge were the Eastcote Hill Estate, the Manor Farm Estate, Eastcote Road, Ruislip, and the Hillingdon Mount Estate. A new station was opened at Hillingdon in 1923 to serve this development: 'Only 15 miles from London in a delightful rural district . . . within easy reach of the quaint old market town of Uxbridge.' It also served the Swakeleys estate then being developed at Ickenham by Stedman and Clarke.

The Cedars Estate between Rickmansworth and Chorley Wood was the largest estate the Metropolitan developed. 'An exceptionally attractive residential country estate comprising over 600 acres of beautiful undulating country rising to an altitude of 300 feet. Detached residences of the country house type and of artistic design. Wide and well-made roads. specially designed detached residences embracing all modern and labour saving conveniences £975-£2150.'

And furthest out into the Chilterns was the Weller Estate, which was situated both sides of the line at Amersham station.

Here were the homes 'fit for heroes', if they could afford the repayments. Other estates, by developers not connected with the Metropolitan, followed, and by the end of the 1930s the urbanisation of Middlesex was almost complete. Wembley Park joined with Harrow, Ruislip with Pinner and North Harrow with Rayners Lane. Great new roads were built and the last of the fields succumbed to the builders. The Metropolitan Railway Country Estates had built some 4600 houses by the time the Second World War broke out, and even as late as the 1950s, it was still active.

A day in the country
Before going on to the photographs, a brief mention must be made of the excursions and outings for which Metro-land was famed in the 1920s and 1930s. It was the children who came on those day outings to rural Eastcote and leafy

Metro-land in the Twenties
Along the main line of the Metropolitan's Extension Line into the Chilterns, large houses by today's standards were in process of erection for the businessman and his family — all of whom were expected to use the railway. Many were architect designed by the Company's own man — C. W. Clark. Lord Aberconway constantly referred to him as 'my clarkitect'.

Authors' Collection

LOCAL DATA, &c.

relating to

NEASDEN, WEMBLEY PARK, PINNER, RICKMANSWORTH & CHORLEY WOOD

Districts.

	Distance to Baker Street	Trains each way daily	Journey time to Baker Street	Altitude above sea level	Subsoil
	miles		minutes	feet	
Neasden	6	188	11	127	Gravel & Clay
Wembley Park ...	6½	101	11½	234	Clay
Pinner	11¼	35	23	163-230	Clay
Rickmansworth ...	17½	40	30	150-270	Gravel & Chalk
Chorley Wood ...	19½	36	38	368	Gravel & Chalk

	Local Rates	Gas per therm	Water	Electric Light
Neasden	16/1	10d.	8 % on Rates	6d. less 5%
Chalk Hill ...	15/6	10d.	7 % plus extras plus 60 %	7d.
Pinner	9/6	1/2	7 % ditto	10d.
Rickmansworth ...	13/6	1/6	7½ %	10d.
Chorley Wood ...	10/10	1/8	7½ %	10d.

Hanbury, Tomsett & Co., Kensal Rise, N.W.10.

TYPICAL METRO-LAND HOMESTEAD.

COUNTRY HOMES IN METRO-LAND.

HOWEVER beautiful and healthy a country-side may be, it is unfitted for the erection of dwelling-houses until a certain amount of preparatory work has been accomplished on the land. An approved scheme, for instance, has to be laid down ; roads must be made, a drainage system planned and constructed, water, gas and electric light laid on, etc.

These preliminaries, which occupy far more thought, time and labour than appear on the surface, form part of what is termed the "development of an Estate," and have a considerable influence on its character.

It is fortunate then for their prospective purchasers that the large, new residential estates at Chorley Wood, Rickmansworth, Pinner, Wembley Park, Neasden, etc., are controlled by such an organisation as the Metropolitan Railway Country Estates, Ltd., whose Board consists of several of the Directors and the General Manager of the Metropolitan Railway Company, with their experts.

A perusal of the details on the following pages will show that the skilful and experienced management, under which the Estates are being developed, is studying to combine to their fullest extent all that is beautiful in housing architecture with the natural beauties of the site.

Further information readily supplied by H. GIBSON. The Metropolitan Railway Country Estates, Ltd., Baker Street Station, N.W.1.

Ruislip years before, who later became the home owners.

'Metro-land, London's nearest countryside . . . charm and peace awaits you and those who visit it for the first time are enchanted by its beauty, and those who visit it never lose their love for it.'

The Company issued a series of booklets covering suitable places for a Sunday school treat. These included the famous Pavilion at Eastcote, where 'well over a million and a half kiddies and grown-ups have spent the day of their lives over the past 30 years'. Or out to Rickmansworth where, after a day's rambling armed with one of the Metropolitan's very long running country walks series of booklets, you could enjoy a 'dainty cream ice, tea and Kunzle cakes at Beasley's Restaurant or Ye Red Spider. Or take a strawberry tea at

the Cocoa Tree next to Pinner's ancient parish church. The Cocoa Tree, like The Pavilion at Eastcote, was a temperance establishment and had a sign depicting a tree with cups of cocoa hanging from the branches.

Chorley Wood was for the more ambitious. 'Its spreading gorse-clad common and its pure bracing atmosphere . . . an ideal spot for all lovers of a breezy open country'. The children could be amused at Younger's Retreat with its donkeys, or you could spend a whole weekend at the Stagg Farm Holiday Camp over at Flaunden for 7/6d.

Amersham was more for the walker, and in the evening there was a wide variety of hotels, including The Crown, where you could dance to the music of Henry Hall on an electric gramophone.

Metro-land offered golf courses

Metro-land Calendar for 1923
No brash, half clothed ladies for the calendars of the 1920s, but an elegant coloured reminder of country homes in Metro-land. The calendar carried a 'Metro Message' for each month of the year.

H. V. Borley

'I'm happy when I'm hiking . . .'
A popular song of the 1930s that caught the spirit of the new age of freedom, when women had the vote at last and it seemed a good idea to use the only free day of the week to walk the Chiltern footpaths. The Met issued walk itineraries from the start of the century.

Authors' Collection

'We do like to be Beside the Seaside'

Through trains direct to the sea attracted large crowds from Metroland, including large organised parties. This picture shows the Metropolitan Railway Annual Juniors' Outing to Hastings 1910. No swimming trunks then. The Edwardian youths wore full waistcoats and dark suits, even though they placed their boaters at a rakish angle for the photographer. All departments were represented.

An excursion the previous year from Verney Junction direct to Ramsgate and Margate was included in the summer programme operated in conjunction with the South Eastern and Chatham Railway.

above: H. V. Borley
below: Sigrist Collection

in plenty — from the famous clubs like Moor Park, to the small courses, where in the early 1930s 'ladies were admitted'. Courses at Neasden, Wembley Park and Harrow were sold in the 1920s and were built over, but there were still plenty of links further out — Northwick Park survived until 1939.

'To the City man', said the advertisements in the period soon after the 1914-18 War, 'the Metropolitan is the short cut to the nearest golf course. From his office he can step in at any of the Met stations close by, and be taken in a few minutes by electric train to the links without a change. The train service is rapid, inexpensive and luxurious.'

Golf, donkey rides, a day in the country and a walk over the Chiltern Hills, then a house on a new hygienic estate away from the noise and dust of London. A house with stained glass windows in the hall, a front garden with neat lawn and rose trees, a parade of shops by the Metropolitan station and a tennis court or two and a golf course down the road. This was the message of Metro-land.

Get out the picnic case, fill the Thermos flask, and don't forget the 'Brownie' Camera. Join us at Baker Street Station in one of those brown trains with the round topped doors. We're off down memory lane again to spend another day in Metro-land.

'The Kaiser's up to something But in the meantime, before we enjoy the new war that's just around the corner, let's go out on Bank Holiday Monday to the Chilterns. Tear off a handbill as you pass Baker Street station. There's bound to be some extra trains and cheap fares'.

H. V. Borley

Baker Street to Harrow

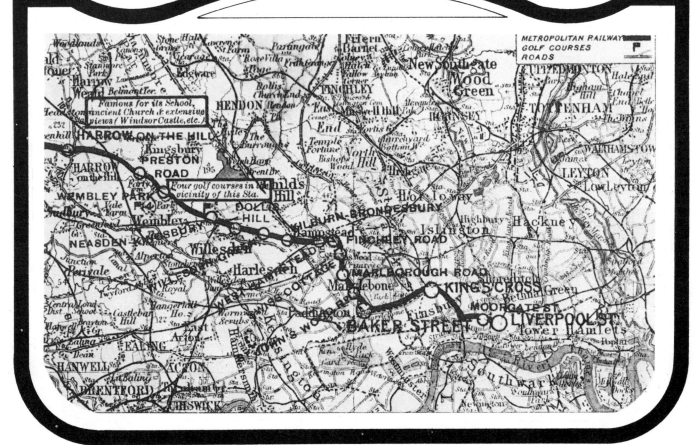

'One hardly connects the Metropolitan
Railway and its underground connections
with golf, but an excellent poster, just
issued, draws attention to the fact that
quite a number of golf links are situated
conveniently to the Extension Line
of the Metropolitan Railway.'

Railway Magazine April 1910

Baker Street: 'Right-away to Metro-land'
A 'C' class locomotive just about to depart for Aylesbury at the turn of the century. The 'C' class were ordered from Neilson and Co. by Sir Edward Watkin, the Met's Chairman, in 1891. At the same time he also placed an order for very similar engines for his South Eastern Railway.

London Transport

Finchley Road: Into the light of day
  'Once past Finchley Road, we
    emerge on open country
  . . . there is no wide belt of
    manufactories'.
(Early guide to the 'Extension line')
But in 1898, when this picture was
taken of 'Medusa', one of the early
batch of 'A' class engines built for
the original Metropolitan line, the
area around Finchley Road was
already being developed and the
nearest countryside was at
Willesden.

  Locomotive Club of Great Britain

**West Hampstead: The coming of
the Great Central**
The original station, with one of
the Beyer Peacock condensing
engines of the 'B' type built in
1880. No. 58 had a comparatively
short life, being sold to Fraser and
Company for scrap in 1911.
  Work is under way in the background for laying new tracks for
the Metropolitan trains. The
existing lines in the foreground will
become the tracks for the Great
Central trains into Marylebone.

  *Leicester Museums, Art
  Galleries, and Records Service*

Kilburn: Sunday morning spectacular

No doubt there were many people late for church and chapel on this winter morning in the early days of the First World War. But it's not every day that a huge steel bridge is swung out over the Edgware Road. This picture was taken in January 1915, when the railway was being quadrupled between Finchley Road and Wembley Park. Mr Willcox, the Civil Engineer of the Metropolitan Railway was in charge. On Sunday 30 May the new bridge was officially tested by running eight locomotives, four on each track over the bridge. The combined weight was over 400 tons.

London Borough of Brent

Willesden Green: By eight-wheeler to Harrow

London is growing and the new houses under construction are in Dartmouth Road, they could be rented from £70 to £220 per year. The engine is one of the Beyer Peacock type, No. 34. She was sold to Bradford Corporation in 1905 and became No. 2 'Milner' when working on the Nidd Valley Light Railway. In January 1914 she was sold again, to the Welsh Granite Company and worked around the quarries of distant Penmaenmawr until 1939.

London Transport

Willesden Green: Rest period

One of the second batch of electric locomotives delivered in 1906 and equipped with British Thomson-Houston electrical gear. No. 11 is seen here waiting to take a local train to Baker Street one day in 1908.

Len's of Sutton

Willesden green: Urban classical 1932
Despite the horse cab (was it just there to impress the photographer?) the date of this picture is about 1932. One of the posters on the far left advertises a comfortable afternoon at the Willesden Empire Cinema where Clark Gable and Helen Hayes are appearing in 'White Sister'. The lettering along the top of the station is still there today. Note the wires and tracks of the North Metropolitan tramways passing the station. The whole scene is in contrast to the tiny halts of outer Metro-land at this time.

London Transport

Willesden Green: Cottage orné
The original station buildings dating from 1879. In the 'Suburban Homes of London' published in 1881, the Willesden area is described:

'Although at present there are so few houses in this locality, many buildings are in course of formation; and no doubt, considering the desirability of the site and its easy communication with London, many more will follow.'

London Transport

Neasden: Down at 'The Old Spotted Dog'
'The Old Spotted Dog' was a favourite
place for workers from the new
Metropolitan Railway works after a hard
day in the repair shops.
London Borough of Brent

Neasden: A cab at the door
When this station opened in 1880, Neasden hamlet was so small that the name of the nearest village, Kingsbury, was also used. But by the 1900s the place was growing up on the edge of London and the cabs are waiting to take commuters, who have travelled down from London on one of the new electric trains, to their houses up on Dudding Hill.

London Borough of Brent

Neasden: The Metropolitan Works
A picture of about 1920. The power station and reservoir date from 1904-5, being built for the Baker Street-Uxbridge electrification scheme. In the background is the old Dog Lane bridge before the North Circular Road was cut. Some new housing development is going on at the left centre, beyond the railway works. The Great Central Railway Sidings are on the top right, whilst the land at the bottom of the picture is on the edge of the Chalk Hill estate which had just been purchased by the Metropolitan for housing.

London Transport

Neasden: Up she goes!
A Metropolitan steam crane, put through its paces for the benefit of Metropolitan directors, lifts an empty goods wagon with commendable ease. The time is probably in the 1920s.

Authors' Collection

Neasden: Interior of the old saw mills

A constant, but not unpleasant noise of the power-saws was always to be heard here. Also at Neasden works was the Brass Foundry, the Coppersmiths (under a Mr Judd), and the Gas Works. Gas made here was fed to special cylinders beneath the carriages for supplying the lights in the compartments in the days before electric light. Mr Judd upon retiring, bought 'The Leather Bottle' public house deep in the heart of the Metro-land Chilterns near Wendover.

Sigrist Collection

Neasden: The 18th Century on wheels

The inaugural run of the Liverpool Street to Aylesbury Pullman Car service took place in May 1910, when luncheon to celebrate the event was held at the 'George', Aylesbury. It gave hours of almost non-stop dining!

The decoration of the Met's two Pullman cars was 'that of the latter part of the 18th century' and on each of the eight glass-topped tables was a 'tiny portable electrollier of a very chaste design', bell pushes in handy positions; while above each blind was an ormolu baggage rack and 'finely chased, gilded panel'.

The first train left Aylesbury for Aldgate at 8.30am, while the last, full of pleasure-soaked revellers, left Baker Street for Aylesbury at 11.35pm.

This photograph shows what is almost certainly the special train used for the press run in 1910.

Both Pullman cars ('Galatea' and 'Mayflower') plus the Rothschild Saloon — the special carriage used for directors and special guests — are coupled together with some of the carriages then used on the 'main line' service. The Rothschild Saloon was originally two vehicles built to convey Lord Rothschild and his retinue from Wendover to London. The carriages were re-built as one vehicle about 1905 and fitted out with furniture from Maples. The carriage was last used for the special train which carried London Transport members to Quainton Road in 1935 for a tour of inspection of the Brill and Verney sections — a trip on which the decision was made to close those far flung lines of the Met. The Pullman service was withdrawn in October 1939.

H. Gael

Approaching Neasden
This picture was taken just after the First World War ended and shows the Metropolitan and Great Central lines before the surrounding countryside became part of London.

London Transport

Neasden: Right-angled turn

The Metropolitan had few accidents, but shunting mishaps do happen! Here a train of 'MV' cars has left the 'straight and narrow' at Neasden sidings. Car 497 was one of the 1920-23 'Dreadnoughts' built for steam services, but converted for running with the 'MV' cars of 1927.

H. Gael

Neasden: Early 'camel-back'

The 'camel-back' locomotives went into service in 1906 and carried these rather ugly destination blinds for a few years before somebody thought of replacing them with neat and smaller signs made of iron. The locos took 'main line' trains as far as Harrow, where steam locomotives took over for the journey to the Chilterns. An electric locomotive survived as a shunter on the Moorgate-Finsbury Park 'Great Northern and City' tube line until 1948. When she was withdrawn on 4 March it is said that she was destined to be preserved, but was broken up by mistake.

H. Gael

Wembley Park: The boys of the old brigade

There was nothing nicer than a day out in the acres of old Wembley Park. Plenty of space to march and play the bugles without upsetting the neighbours! Here the vicar of Wembley village poses with the Boys' Brigade about 1907, not long before Watkin's Folly was removed. This great Tower of London never rose more than one stage and the crowds that were expected to make it a rival attraction to Paris never came.

London Borough of Brent

44

Neasden: All dressed for the occasion

The completion of the Harrow and Uxbridge branch in 1904 was an important event. So the official opening train of 30 June 1904 was specially decorated. Here 'E' class engine No. 1 (the original No. 1 was smashed in an accident) of 1898 is about to be backed on to the train of eight-wheeled carriages and the Rothschild Saloon. But there is time for the crew and some of the Metropolitan's 'top brass' to pose for the camera.

H. Gael

Wembley Park: The last leg

After a visit to Paris in 1889, Sir Edward Watkin came back inspired to build a rival to the Eiffel Tower at Wembley. All London would come to see the dramatic views from the top. A Metropolitan Tower Company was formed and a competition with a prize of 500 guineas launched. The winners were a London firm, MacLaren and Dunn. After 18 months' work and 1,800 tons of concrete and steel, only the first stage was reached before the money ran out. Despite the attractions of the circus, Buffalo Bill's Wild West Show and other displays, the crowds weren't interested.

'Speculation is rising', said the

Harrow Observer on 14 December 1906, 'that the Wembley Tower Company is proposing to demolish the tower . . . the majority of people will find pleasure in the removal of this unsightly blot on the landscape'.

On 13 September 1907 the press reported that the tower had gone. The last leg was blown up with a special explosive called 'Roburite'. The work was carried out by securing the leg to neighbouring trees by means of huge chain links. There was a loud explosion and the vibrations were felt for many miles. This picture shows the demolition contractor's tents and vehicles shortly before the final blow was dealt.

London Borough of Brent

Wembley Park: The world comes to Wembley

'It will be a city of peep-shows and playhouses, cafes and restaurants, massed bands and movies — every class will be catered for, every taste, every desire for novelty, and the latest thrill, for the world has been ransacked for its side shows.' So the *Sunday Times* wrote about the British Empire Exhibition at Wembley in 1924.

Conceived as an idea by Lord Strathcona before the First World War, the great exhibition rose on the grasslands of Wembley Park where the Tower had stood and golf had been played. It became the largest concrete 'city' in the world. Yet despite its popularity and its ideals celebrating the British Empire and its achievements, it was really a final show of the Empire before the sun began to go down. Its sprawl of buildings was old-fashioned looking. It was a glorious celebration of the past.

King George V's opening address 'I declare the British Empire Exhibition open and pray by the blessing of God that it may conduce the unity and prosperity of my people and the peace and well-being of the world.'

on St George's Day 1924 was the first time the monarch had spoken on the BBC. The exhibition was a success and was repeated, perhaps less profitably, in 1925. Thousands came to Metro-land for the first time and many came again and again to see the exhibition and to explore the beauties of the local countryside.

Authors' Collection

Australian Pavilion

Wembley Park: The British Empire Exhibition 1924

The Metropolitan Railway can be seen at the bottom right hand corner, beside the vast amusement park. The line curling round to the left is the LNER loop serving the newly built Stadium. The large white buildings are the Palaces of Engineering and Arts, with the 'never-stop' railway curving in front of them.

Authors' Collection

Canons Park: Mid-day shuttle

For a short period after the opening of the new branch on 10 December 1932, the countryside at the northern end of the line remained open. This single car electric train is passing the wooded acres of historic Canons Park in 1934. Car No. 69 with its sister No. 46 were built in 1910 from parts salvaged from two early electric saloon cars that had been involved in a serious accident. The compartment shuttle cars worked with saloon trailers on the Harrow and Uxbridge service between 1910 and 1918, then on the old Addison Road line in London until the opening of the Watford Branch in 1925, when they ran between Rickmansworth and Watford. In the early 1930s cars Nos. 46 and 69 came on to the Wembley Park-Stanmore branch. No. 46 was scrapped in 1938 and 69 was withdrawn in 1939 when the Bakerloo Line took over operation of the Stanmore run.

Locomotive Club of Great Britain

Stanmore; preparing the new route.
The new line received Royal Assent
on 4 June 1930 and was hailed as a
means of giving employment to
many hundreds of men. The contractors were Walter, Scott and
Middleton Limited and the work
involved the diversion of the Wealdstone Brook between Wembley
Park and Preston Road stations and
the digging of some deep cuttings at
Kingsbury and south of Stanmore.
The contractors' line can be seen in
this picture crossing unspoiled
countryside. Within a few years the
whole area was to become
completely built up and the old,
muddy and impassable Honeypot
Lane became a modern traffic
artery with modern factories and
low-priced suburban housing.

Authors' Collection

Stanmore: The inquisitive grocer
Stanmore Broadway was still a
village street with a few modern
shops when the Metropolitan's
photographer called one day in
1931 to take pictures. The new
terminus was under construction
just down the road. Designed by
the Railway's own architect,
C. W. Clark, it was built in the
'suburban villa' style he used at
Watford and Croxley Green, and
later at Northwood Hills.

Houses were being offered on the
Park Farm Estate for £1425, 'With
all British materials . . . hot water
radiators in the main bedroom, hall
and landing.'

Authors' Collection

Preston Road: Electric goods

Not all Metropolitan goods trains were steam hauled. Heading for the Finchley Road yards is Metropolitan-Vickers locomotive 'Michael Faraday'. In the background are houses on the Woodcock Dell estate. Incidentally, the motor-man has forgotten to change the destination plate, so the train appears to be heading for Aylesbury!

H. Gael

Northwick Park: Fast train to the Chilterns

Metropolitan-Vickers locomotive 'John Lyon' with a train of 'Dreadnought' carriages in about 1931. The 'Metro-Vick' electric locomotives were built in 1921-3 and some of the class incorporated parts of the old 'camel back' and 'sardine can' electric locomotives.

Following a meeting of the Met's traffic committee on 18 March 1927, it was decided to name the 20 new locomotives after people connected with places served by the Railway. The first named engine appeared on Monday 3 October 1927. The locomotive in this picture took part in the Metropolitan Railway Centenary parade of 1963. She was broken up at Neasden in 1974, but the name plates are preserved. The names of the 20 locomotives were as follows:—

1. John Lyon 2. Oliver Cromwell (re-named Thomas Lord in 1953). 3. Sir Ralph Verney. 4. Lord Byron. 5. John Hampden (now preserved at the London Transport Museum at Covent Garden). 6 William Penn. 7. Edmund Burke. 8. Sherlock Holmes. 9. John Milton. 10. William Ewart Gladstone. 11. George Romney. 12. Sarah Siddons. (This locomotive is in use as a service engine and was taken all the way to Co. Durham in 1975 to take part in the 150th Anniversary of Railways display. She can still be seen with trucks, travelling along the old Meotropolitan 'Extension Line'). 13. Dick Whittington. 14. Benjamin Disraeli. 15. Wembley 1924 (put on display at the British Empire Exhibition with a specially cut-away side). 16. Oliver Goldsmith. 17. Florence Nightingale. 18. Michael Faraday. 19. John Wycliffe. 20. Sir Christopher Wren.

Locomotive Club of Great Britain

Northwick Park: New trains for Watford

One of the 'MW' class compartment cars with train passing the Northwick Park estate. Introduced in 1927 and followed by the 'MV' motor cars, the trains ran with some trailers converted from steam 'Dreadnought' carriages. The last compartment train, then known as the 'T' stock, ran in 1962 on the Metropolitan Line.

The Northwick Park estate was built in the early 1920s on land once owned by the Churchill family. The station opened on 26 June 1923 and was named after the Churchill estate in Gloucestershire. Houses were laid out on an estate which developers (The Lord Northwick Trust Estates) claimed was a unique example of town planning. 'The Palaestra' recreation club offered tennis, bowls and a 'large tea room and dance hall'.

London Transport

Harrow

The original approach to the station from London as it was on 31 May 1902. The engine in charge of this train is 'C' class No. 70, built by Neilson and Co in 1891. The Great Central trains also used the same pair of tracks at this time. But work is under way widening the line and the Metropolitan trains will shortly use the lines to be laid over to the left. The 'Dutch' style building nearing completion on the right is still a well known landmark to passengers waiting for trains at Harrow. The trees on the left have long since gone, the bridge rebuilt and a row of shops constructed along it.

Locomotive Club of Great Britain

Harrow: Change-over point
One of the 'camel back' electric locomotives of 1906 and an 'E' class steam engine at the service point just outside Harrow station. After electrification of the line to Uxbridge, Harrow station was enlarged and Verney Junction and Aylesbury trains changed locomotives here, although some steam passenger trains still continued to Willesden Green for the change-over until the First World War. The coaling stage and siding at Harrow were little used after the extension of the electric rails to Rickmansworth in 1925.

A. W. Croughton Collection

Harrow: Uxbridge steam
Although built as an electric line, The Harrow and Uxbridge branch opened in 1904 with a service of steam trains until the power station and other equipment was ready the following year. Here is a rare view of a train from Uxbridge just entering Harrow station. The locomotive is 'A' class 'Medusa', one of the first batch of condensing locomotives built for the pioneer line between Bishopsgate and Farringdon Street in 1864. The old Harrow station of 1880 was enlarged and extra track constructed in 1908.

F. M. Gates

Willesden Green to Chorley Wood & Uxbridge

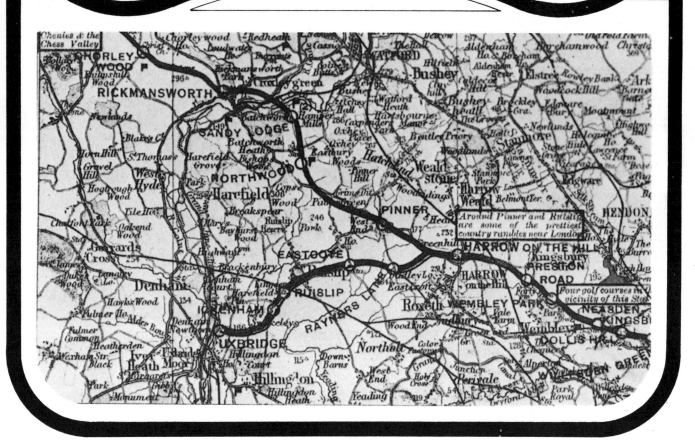

'Weekends in Metro-land, what
delightful days they were! I think
over those years I took refreshment
at all the little country pubs, and I
well remember *all* the beers were
good — or was I thirsty?'

Former Metropolitan Railway employee

Rayners Lane: The old farmhouse
Here Farmer' Rayner lived and
gave his name to what for centuries
had been Bourne or Pinner Lane.
As late as 1929 the area was
described as 'still awaiting development'.

London Borough of Harrow

Rayners Lane: The building of Harrow Garden Village

'Good progress has been made in the last few months with the new Harrow Garden Village which is being planned under the auspices of the MRCE. It is based, so to speak, upon the station at Rayners Lane. The planning is on general lines and already a flying start has been made in the direction of West Harrrow'.

The elms and the telegraph poles and the road surface are the final reminders of the rural days. The houses are going up in Village Way and the first parades of new 'Tudor' style shops rise up the hill towards the station.

Authors' Collection

Rayners Lane: 'We'll build a homestead that's just made for two'
E. S. Reid's Harrow Garden Village estate was one of the most popular places to settle down in Metro-land. Smart neo-Tudor or similar style houses are being built here for £895 and no doubt the young couple are looking forward to moving in with their smart new furniture from Drages or Maples. 'On this estate houses are moved to retain the trees and hedges. The first residents have taken up their abode and with the Spring it is expected that their numbers will increase', said E. S. Reid's brochure of 1932.

Authors' Collection

Rayners Lane: Booking office
You had to stand on the narrow strip of footpath beside muddy Rayners Lane to get your ticket to town in 1930. This hut is typical of many of the Metropolitan halts. Rayners Lane opened in 1906 and was the junction for the District Railway to Ealing and London.

Mr A. Joce of Eastcote recalls waiting for a train home in the 'rush hour' before the First World War. 'The air was filled with the singing of countless larks, and the scent of the hayfields. The only signs of life were the distant barns of Rayners Farm on the way to Pinner.' In the background of this picture are the first houses at Rayners Lane. They were built for £895 or so by A. Robinson and one of the inducements to visit his estate was a refund on your ticket if you called at his estate office.

London Transport

Eastcote: Ploughing for victory
During the First World War, the
Metropolitan Railway began culti-
vating the spare strips of land it
owned beside the line from Rayners
Lane to Uxbridge. The crops grown
were mainly vegetables which went
towards supplementing the diet of
the railwaymen. The cultivation
was undertaken in a professional
way. Here a ploughman is struggling
with the thick Middlesex clay on
land beside Eastcote halt. In the
distance to the far right you can see
some of the first pioneer suburban
houses in Elm Avenue. The land
where the cultivation is going on is
now occupied by an electric sub-
station and a builder's yard.
Authors' Collection

Eastcote: The day of their lives
'How long have we got to wait, Mum?'

There were few London children 50 years or more ago who hadn't come out to rural Eastcote and the delights of a donkey derby, electric swings and sports at Captain Bayly's 'Pavilion' Pleasure Grounds in Field End Road. As many as 4000 could be provided with 1/6d lunches or teas under cover, so the people waiting here for the gates to open won't be too worried if it rains some of the time.

The sign for 'The Ship Inn' here advertised another popular spot — although this inn was along the road between Eastcote village and the future Northwood Hills. 'The Ship' had an open fronted pavilion and there was a dance every Wednesday and Saturday with a 'live orchestra'.

London Transport

Eastcote: In the bleak mid-winter
The windswept, wet fields at Eastcote looking towards Rayners Lane
in about 1915. One of the two-car
shuttle trains that worked the
service from Uxbridge to Harrow
is passing the ground frame box
which controlled a small siding over
to the right. The leading car of the
train is one of the two compartment cars constructed from parts
salvaged after a serious accident to
two of the original saloon cars in
1910.

'All one could see from Eastcote
station looking south was about
three houses and The Pavilion in
the spread of fields and open
spaces', said an old Eastcote
resident to one of the authors of
this book.

Authors' Collection

Eastcote: Wartime harvest
Metropolitan Railway staff are busy
harvesting potatoes which have
been grown on spare land at Eastcote as part of the War effort. For
this is 1916, and there is little food
about — especially for railwaymen.
All along the railway to Uxbridge,
the surplus lands were ploughed up
and crops grown. Note the typical
Metropolitan booking hut and the
signs advertising fast trains to town.
The small building with the
chimney was for many years a cafe.
The site of the harvesting is now a
garden centre.

Authors' Collection

Eastcote: A deal in wild duck

So peaceful were the roads in Eastcote village in the 1900s that there
was time to stand and sell a duck
to a friend. The man on the right
probably shot the ducks along the
banks of the River Pinn which
flows behind the trees on the left.
Or he could have got them at
Ruislip Reservoir. The children are
walking along the edge of the Eastcote House estate, the most important large house in the village — the
home of the Hawtry-Deane family.

The lane branching off to the left
by the white posts is Joel Street
which leads past the green houses
and high walls of Haydon Hall.
Although heavy traffic and pave-
ments have taken the place of the
empty highway and the grass
verges, the scene today is otherwise
little changed at this spot.

Helen Hoare Collection

**Eastcote: A Tudor home in
Metro-land**

Entrance to the St Lawrence Drive
estate at Eastcote village, October
1933. Messrs Comben and Wakeling
built high-class neo-Tudor houses
like this in many parts of Metro-
land. This estate was built on the
site of 'The Sigers,' once the house
of a Bank of England Governor.
Apparently the Eastcote children
had a wonderful time building
castles with the bricks or risking
their lives 'mountaineering' on the
wooden scaffolding round the
unfinished houses. Yet down the
road to the left there were still part-
ridges in the coverts and woods
along the banks of the River Pinn.
The cart in this picture is probably
one of William Clarke's, the Ruislip
hauler. He carried builders' supplies
from Eastcote and Ruislip sidings
to estates all over the area.

Helen Hoare Collection

Ruislip Manor — Builder's train.
'Reached in less time than it takes to read the evening paper.' 'FREE, TONIGHT! BRING YOUR FRIENDS TO SEE THE GREAT FIREWORKS AND SEARCH-LIGHT DISPLAY AT RUISLIP MANOR'. *The Evening News* 30 September 1933. To many of those who came, it meant the start of a new life in one of Geo. Ball's compact new neo-Tudor semi or terraced houses. But the fireworks were also the funeral pyre of the old rural Metro-land. After that the houses swiftly covered the elm-lined fields for mile after mile. And to the very few, those searchlights were a grim portent of seven years later when they were to pierce the night skies again seeking out the enemy bombers.   *Helen Hoare Collection*

Ruislip

A 1933 advertisement for the Bowers estate, which was just south of the Metropolitan railway. 'In a delightful part of this rural district and within easy reach of the old-world town of Uxbridge.'

Authors' Collection

AT LAST—A 'QUALITY' HOUSE AT LOW COST

HERE is your chance—seize it! A real worth-while "quality" seven-roomed house for £695 Freehold. No road charges, no legal costs, and no stamp fees to pay! Built of the finest materials; thoughtfully planned; excellently appointed, with rooms throughout that possess that cheery touch of brightness that means everything. Inner fittings and equipment include—totally enclosed porcelain enamelled bath; magnificent tiled fireplaces; chromium plated fittings throughout; beautifully tiled kitchens and bathrooms; constant hot water supply; electric fittings and shades, etc., etc.

The Ruislip Station Estate, on which these delightful houses are located, has everything in its favour. It can be

reached, from Town, in less time than it takes to read your evening paper. On all sides are green fields and pleasant hedgerows. The climate is mild and enjoyable; the air is healthy and invigorating, whilst unlimited facilities for outdoor recreation obtain and particularly liberal educational and shopping facilities exist.

Why not go further into the matter—it will pay you! Write to-day, or telephone Ruislip 217 or 626, for free travelling voucher from any London station and for illustrated descriptive booklet. The houses can be inspected any day, including Sundays, and our representatives, who are always available, will readily answer any question or explain any point without the slightest obligation on your part to buy.

£695 FREEHOLD

H. L. BOWERS, RUISLIP STATION ESTATE, MIDDX.

SAY YOU SAW IT IN "METRO-LAND."

Ruislip: Village in transition

By the 1920s Ruislip's village street was already half urbanised. The boundary fence on the left is part of 'The Poplars' Tea Gardens, soon to close for ever. The building with the turret is Fabb's Hotel and restaurant. Here one could 'dine and taste fine wines and dance to a three-piece orchestra'. The trees in the distance are part of the grounds of Park House.

Helen Hoare Collection

RUISLIP VILLAGE.

WESTMINSTER BANK LIMITED

Ruislip: Pioneers of suburbia

In 1903, a year before the line to Uxbridge opened, King's College, Cambridge agreed to sell some of its land at Ruislip for building. This early picture shows how rough the estate roads could be. Nanny must have had a very difficult job with her young 'charges' as she paused to talk to the gentleman from the semi-detached houses over to the right in what is now Manor Road.

Helen Hoare Collection

Ruislip: Swing high and low at The Poplars

So popular did The Poplars become that Mr Weedon opened a sports field and refreshment tents near King's End Farm along the road to Ickenham and the GWR/GCR Joint station. About 1912-13 he got Fred Parnum to set to music some verses by H. St George. 'Neath the shade of the Ruislip Poplars' and 'The Poplars Waltz' became 'pop' music hits of the day! The sheets were sold at Ruislip rather like tourist records are sold today at stately homes. And like all 'pop' tunes, the lyrics were appalling verses that were best sung! However, here's a verse and chorus from one song that describes the swings and roundabouts seen in this picture of the Poplars Sports Field.

Helen Hoare Collection

Neath the shade of the Ruislip Poplars;
You'll notice soon a very lively batch
Find their way to the sporting fields to play
at tennis or a cricket match
And coconut shies, quoits or swings
Delight customers by the score
After all the games and the fun is done,
You will find you can eat some more.
Chorus:
So you spend the day with Rose you see,
At the Poplars where sweet Bluebell serves the tea.
And Lily's white hands brings cakes and jam,
And don't they enjoy Miss Pansy's cold lamb!
The jellies and custards by Poppy and May.
And the cream brought by Daisy as sweet as Hay.
Its a very short distance by rail on the Met,
And at the gate you'll find waiting, sweet Violet.

Ruislip: All roads lead to The Poplars

This was Ruislip's most famous spot for refreshments and fun in the dreamy summer days, when it never rained, before 1914. 'Come to breezy Ruislip, the garden of Middlesex, with its magnificent woods and splendid scenery. One can walk for miles through beautiful pasture land covered with wild flowers. Toys, sweets, and high teas.' The enterprising owner of the Poplars, George Weedon, had a brilliant publicity idea in 1913. He dressed the waitresses in green and white outfits, with white shoes and caps. Each girl wore an imitation flower and her flower 'name' — Poppy, Rose, Violet, etc. Here they are with Mr Weedon in front of the house which stood at the junction of Ruislip High Street and Ickenham Road.

Helen Hoare Collection

Ickenham: At the forge

Every village had a forge; it was the equivalent of today's service station. The Ickenham blacksmith worked from a small building near the 'Coach & Horses' public house. He was Llewellyn Wood and he advertised 'horses shod on approved principles'.

London Borough of Hillingdon

Ickenham: The village halt

Few places on the line to Uxbridge were more picturesque or remote than Ickenham. At first there was no station and it was only after the villagers protested to the local council that the Metropolitan opened a primitive halt on 25 September 1905. The platforms were not lengthened to take six-car trains until the 1920s. This picture was taken in January 1906. The corrugated iron waiting huts survived until 1971. To the left amid the trees are the barns of old Glebe Farm. Whilst in the distance the approach road to the bridge that carries the way to ancient Ickenham manor house is still shored up because the new embankment has been slipping in the winter rain. The train is composed of BTH electric saloons. The front two vehicles are third class and the rear car a first.

The picture was taken by S. W. A. Newton, the Leicester photographer, when he was recording the building of the Great Central and Great Western Joint Railway line as it passed through the fields near the Metropolitan branch between Ickenham and Ruislip.

Leicester Museums

Ickenham: A rural Arcadia

Hard to believe that, although the church and ornamental pump are still there, this road junction in Ickenham village is packed with heavy traffic and suburban shops. Just visible through the arches of the pump is one of the earliest local road signs. In 1909 the Ickenham Parish Council asked for a 7mph speed limit through the village!

The village children have all turned up to pose for the photographer, who probably came from Watford. The rural days, when the only sounds were the birds singing and the occasional electric train on the new Met railway line, seemed set to go on for ever. Then, suddenly, it was August 1914.

London Borough of Hillingdon

Ickenham: The rising suburb 1933
Looking down Swakeleys Road
near Thornhill Road. The houses
under construction on the left are
being built along what is to become
the east bound carriageway of the
new arterial road. The elms along
the middle of the picture will soon
be felled and big steel lamp standards will go up along the edges of
the road. This is progress 1930s
style and typical of how the narrow
and picturesque lanes of old
Middlesex changed in a few years
to busy London suburbs.

London Borough of Hillingdon

**Ickenham: A bright new home in
Metro-land**
The ancient Middlesex countryside
basks in the summer sun as workmen hurry to finish another road of
semi-detached houses. This is a
scene that could have been anywhere in Metro-land between the
Wars. A bright new semi-detached
house like this could be yours for
£595. You paid £25 down and then
weekly payments of 12/6d. There
were 'easiwork' cabinets in the
kitchen and an 'Ideal' boiler; free
light fittings and sometimes the
developers even gave you a cheap
rate season ticket to town for a
year.

The countryside in the picture
here at Ickenham was never built
upon. The War came in 1939 and
then the London Green Belt Plan.

Authors' Collection

Hillingdon: Wartime delivery
Another view from the series of
pictures taken of the 'Dig for
Victory' campaign carried out on
the surplus lands beside the Harrow
and Uxbridge Railway 1914-18.
The train of early electric cars has
stopped near the site of Hillingdon
Station (opened 1923) to pick up a
sack of potatoes from a temporary
'platform'. The countryside here
was then completely open.
Authors' Collection

**The old Belmont Road station
October 1933**
The Piccadilly tube trains began
running through from South Harrow
and Acton Town on 23rd of that
month. A large banner outside
Uxbridge station proclaimed
'Through trains now running to
Piccadilly and West End'. The single
fare to Leicester Square was 7½p!

Northwood to Great Missenden

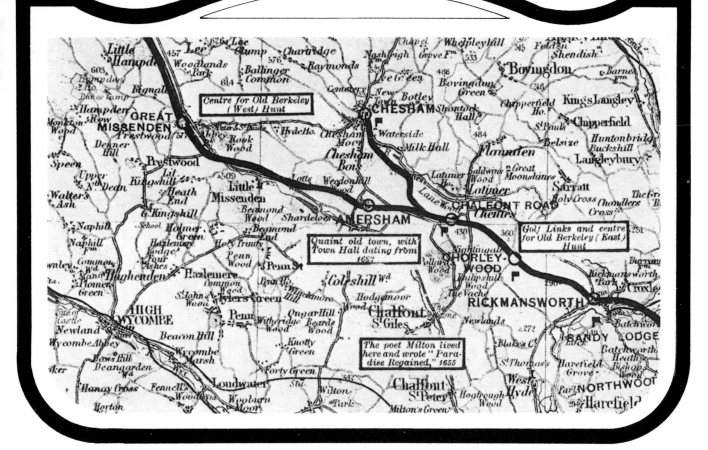

'There has recently been a revival of
Pedestrian-tour tickets, i.e. going
from one station and returning
from another.'

– *Metropolitan Railway
Report, Summer 1921*

STATION ROAD, NORTH HARROW (Pinner). A section of the Western Arterial Road involving widening of the bridge carrying the Metropolitan Railway.
On the left, constructional work progressing in advance of development.

The same thoroughfare completed.

North Harrow: March of time
Station Road and the Metropolitan bridge with the original halt of 1915 on the far left. Before the First World War a local builder, Albert Cutler, was putting up rows of well-built houses along the Pinner Road from Harrow. Work was resumed in the 1920s with more modern styles and soon North Harrow became a large suburb and the halt had to be rebuilt, as well as the railway bridge.

The lower picture shows the new Station road in 1929 — intended as part of 'The Western Arterial Road' from Ealing to Wealdstone. To the left is the gable of the Headstone Hotel and the new parades of shops can be seen under the bridge.

'The changes effected here in the last five years have been as remark-able as any in outer London, the population having more than doubled. On both sides of the line attractive houses are being laid out with pleasant vistas and gardening would seem to be the usual hobby.'

Cutler's houses sold for £720-£950 with the luxury of coke boilers in the kitchen from the early 1920s. 'These boilers are rapidly superseding the old-fashioned dirty and wasteful kitchen range', Mr Cutler announced. Later his houses were more neo-Tudor in design and, in common with some other local builders, offered stained glass in the hallway and in the landing window. There were no less than seven different designs — a cottage (to remind one of the Metro-land countryside that was fast

disappearing), a windmill, a ship in full sail, a sunset, birds and reeds. The design could be ordered with a choice of coloured glasses. By 1934 Cutler had built 1700 houses in the area — 200 houses in 1933 alone. But the local countryside suffered, as even *Metro-land* magazine had to admit:

'It has been necessary to take down many large trees, but it is hoped that the county council will help to replace some of them with new ones.'

By 1933 North Harrow had arrived on the London suburban map. It had a cinema where afternoon teas were served before the Clark Gable picture; an Express Dairy, also W. & E. Long's private dairy where 'milk was supplied direct from six local farms'.

London Borough of Harrow

70

Cecil Park Estate,

PINNER.

(The property of the Metropolitan Railway Surplus Lands Committee.)

Three Reception Rooms and Six Bedrooms. Rent, £65 or £70.

GOOD CLASS SEMI-DETACHED HOUSES to be LET. Rents from £50 to £70.

PLOTS OF LAND
for the erection of Houses of good class are also to be let on Building Lease at moderate ground rents.

THIS ESTATE
is beautifully timbered, charmingly situated, and is within a few minutes walk of Pinner Village and of the Metropolitan Railway Station.

Pinner: The first Metropolitan housing development
Three reception rooms and six bedrooms, friends, and fresh air, were the rewards of moving from the smoke and high rents of inner London to rural Pinner at the turn of the century.

Authors' Collection

Pinner: 'The enchanted ground:
The photographer is standing in
Rayners Lane just where it climbs
the hill to Pinner at what is now the
junction of Suffolk Road and
Whittington Way. The date is
September 1932 and the builders
are hard at work converting the old
countryside and the hedged lane to
suburbia. On the right is a sign for
H. Pickerill houses, which could be
purchased for £790. The small shed
over the grass on the left is the
office of the London and Provincial
Building Co. Another well-known
local builder described the area as
'enchanted ground. Footpaths,
opening out into pleasant land-
scapes from crowded thoroughfares
into the solitude of nature, are very
numerous'.

Borough of Harrow

Pinner: Before the houses came
Clattering along through the peaceful countryside near Pinner before
the area was built up with houses,
is one of the 'C' class locomotives
and a train of eight-wheelers, plus
one of the four-wheeled carriages
built in 1887. The 'C' class engines
were built for the Aylesbury service
by Neilson and Co in 1891 and fitted
with condensing apparatus for use
in the tunnels south of Finchley
Road.

London Transport

Northwood Hills: Site for a new suburb

Joel Street bridge, 1931, and a new sign has just been erected by the railway bridge announcing 'Metropolitan and Great Central Joint Committee Site for new station. Frequent train services will be run to London, City and West End'.

The economic trouble in the North of England at this period sent many enterprising builders south to expanding London, and Northwood Hills was largely a joint creation of a building estate developer called Peachey and the Metroplitan Railway. The Met made Mr Peachey agree to cover any losses the new station might incur in the early years of his estate. But so popular was the area and so rapidly did it grow, that this stipulation was soon withdrawn. The station opened in 1933 and was almost the last of C. W. Clarke's 'domestic style' buildings for the Metropolitan.

London Transport

Northwood: Three cheers for King George and Queen Mary
The crowds have turned out to line the Rickmansworth Road at Northwood for the new suburb's 1911 'imitation' Coronation Parade. The picture was taken from the Metropolitan Railway bridge. The public house and the houses are still there, but the barns on the distance at Hill End Farm are now a dairy depot.

Northwood was predominantly an upper-middle class suburb and the Harrods' lorry on the right was a frequent sight. But it must have had a long and uncomfortable journey all the way from Knightsbridge, along the Harrow Road and the muddy country road from Pinner to Northwood.

London Borough of Hillingdon

WATFORD'S
NEW
RAILWAY

PARTICULARS OF TRAIN
SERVICE AND SEASON
TICKET RATES LONDON
AND CROXLEY GREEN
AND WATFORD.

2nd NOVEMBER, 1925.

Knapp, Drewett & Sons Ltd., Kingston-on-Thames and London.—11424 W.

Watford: The New Railway
The Met reaches Watford. Cover of
the timetable leaflet issued for the
start of the electric line to Watford
in November 1925.

Authors' Collection

Moor Park: The Chiltern gateway

When I was young, there stood among the fields
A lonely station once called Sandy Lodge
Its wooden platform crunched by hobnailed shoes
And this is where the healthier got out

Sir John Betjeman

In 1923 Sandy Lodge was renamed Moor Park and Sandy Lodge. The great classical mansion had been sold by the Ebury family to Lord Levershulme whose Unilever Property Department offered admirable sites in the park for building the house of one's dreams. The mansion and part of the land became the world famous golf course. And few British courses could have had a more sumptuous '19th hole' than this.

'When world conditions compel the advisability of living economically' the rich businessmen were advised, 'the problem which arises is where can one reside and yet retrench whilst maintaining a standard of comfort in a healthy and congenial environment? Moor Park solves this problem!'

Distinctive houses from £1900 freehold, private roads with a gate-keeper to prevent day trippers roaring through on motorcycle combinations or stop street traders shouting their wares, Moor Park was the most luxurious of all the Metro-land estates. 'Here one may enjoy quietude and seclusion (without isolation) with all the amenities of residence in an old English Park, yet without the responsibilities of its ownership.'

'Electric expresses to the City.'

Authors' Collection

Croxley: The new branch takes shape — 1924

Ground clearance taking place for the laying of the southern fork lines near the junction with the main line at Croxley Hall Wood. The new branch cost over £300,000 to build, although some of the money was supplied from the Trade Facilities Act. The engineer was the Metropolitan's E. A. Wilson, and the contractors were Logan and Hemmingway. There is an interesting note in the 1924 edition of *Metro-land* about the Croxley Green Area:

'At Croxley a second village has already sprung up along the half mile of the Watford Road. It is to be hoped that the amenities of the wooded belt on the earthworks of the railway towards Rickmansworth will be preserved as far as possible. Once spoilt, they can never be replaced and spoiling is fatally easy.'

Authors' Collection

Watford: Crossing the river

The Watford branch was designed to 'plug in' to Hertfordshire's largest town and to serve the Cassiobury Park estate, where houses were under construction. But the building of the line proved difficult, particularly near the River Gade and the Grand Union Canal. Extensive pile driving had to be undertaken to shore up the ground. Here steam pile-driving goes on by the river banks.

Authors' Collection

Watford: Keep the flags flying

Put out the flags, clean the coach-work, the buses are entering for Watford Shopping Week.

The Met bus services from Watford terminus to High Street began on 2 November 1927 and connected with each train. The route was via Cassiobury Park Avenue, Hagden Lane, Queens Road, Vicarage Road, St. Mary's Road and the fare was 1d. Later the buses were operated by the Lewis Bus Co, but still carried the fleet name 'Metropolitan'.

Borough of Watford

Watford: Day to celebrate

It is a cold wet November day in 1925. But the flags are out and nothing can dampen the enthusiasm for the opening of the new branch. The special guests, which include Lord Aberconway (Chairman of the Met) and Lord Faringdon (Deputy Chairman of the LNER) are waiting for buses to take them into Watford where a splendid lunch awaits at the Oddfellows Hall. Here the toast was 'The prosperity of Watford'.

The carriage on the right is probably the Rothschild Saloon which formed part of the special train that had left Baker Street at 11.05am, whilst the train on the left is a special from Rickmansworth which carried local councillors and the Mayor of Watford, Alderman M. A. Thorpe.

The *Watford Observer* commented: 'The Metropolitan Railway to Watford . . . is likely to have a much greater effect on the development of the town than is at present realized. Just as trade follows the flag, so population follows the railway.' Advertisements announced all over the town: 'WATFORD'S NEW RAILWAY — METROPOLITAN AND LNER JOINT effort. Latest signals, 140 trains daily; goods facilities for minerals and livestock. Metro lorry

delivery service; cattle pens, horse boxes. Travel the new route . . . easiest and best.' But for all the high hopes, the branch to Watford has never been really popular. The LNER steam trains were never resumed after the General Strike of 1926 and the terminus has seldom seen large crowds. *Borough of Watford*

Rickmansworth: Quick change —
Three minutes later the Metropolitan-Vickers electric locomotive backs on to the train and the couplings and brake hoses are attached.

Authors' Collection

Rickmansworth:
Electric locomotive No. 3 'Sir Ralph Verney'. This locomotive was scrapped in the early 1960s at West Ruislip, where she was a shunter for a short time.

A. W. Croughton Collection

Rickmansworth: Empty stock train in the 1890s.

No. 45 is the latest thing in transport to the Rickmansworth lads. The town has only recently got a direct railway connection with London and watching the trains is still a novelty. The locomotive was built by Beyer Peacock in 1870. She was scrapped in 1906. The signals are of the old Metropolitan balanced semaphore pattern. The station sign would have had white letters against a red tin background.

Locomotive Club of Great Britain

Rickmansworth: Quick change

Just coming off a London-bound train on 8 April 1933, 'H' class locomotive No. 103 (Kerr Stuart and Co 1920) will be replaced by one of the Metropolitan-Vickers electric locomotives within four minutes. The changeover from steam to electric and vice-versa was said to be the quickest operation of its kind anywhere in the world. The practice lasted at Rickmansworth until 1961.

The cab of the train seen just to the left of the lamp-post is the shuttle train that used to run round to Watford via the West curve. Most Rickmansworth people found the buses more frequent — and convenient — because they took you right to the Watford shops, whilst the Metro station was out at Cassiobury Park.

A. W. Croughton Collection

Rickmansworth: In the grounds of Glen Chess

In 1920 Rickmansworth was described as 'an ancient township of narrow streets . . . and the canal where gaudily painted canal boats, each with its patient, plodding horse tugging at the tow rope, can be seen passing to and fro all day long'.

The grounds of Chesswater House were opened to the public on Wednesdays and Thursdays 'thanks to the public spirit of Mr Wilson Young'. Afterwards one could end a perfect afternoon with tea at Ye Red Spider or Beasleys.

Authors' Collection

Great Missenden to Aylesbury

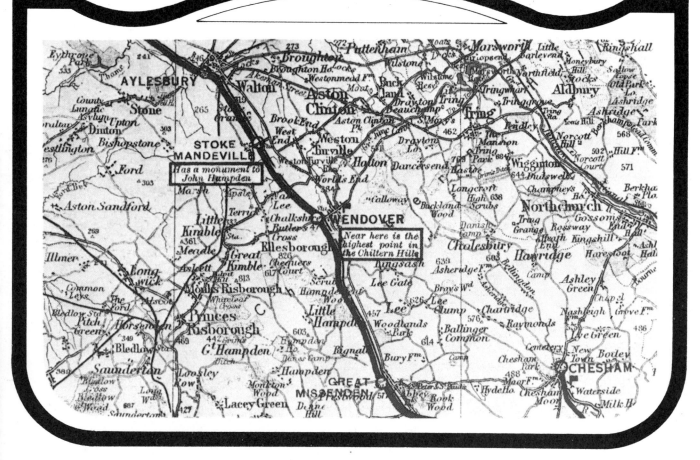

'The antique character of the
medieval villages of the line —
Chenies, Great Missenden,
Wendover etc, has always been carefully
preserved and has remained unchanged
during hundreds of years.'

*'Railway Magazine' quoting Metropolitan
Railway literature in May 1914*

Chorleywood: At your service
Ladies didn't carry the shopping
home from town on the Cedars
Estate 50 years ago. They tele-
phoned their order to Mr Palmer in
Rickmansworth and that very afternoon his van would come bumping
out over the new, wide estate roads
along the valley to deliver fresh
butter, cheese, Chivers Jellies and
packets of Mazawattee Tea.

Rickmansworth Historical Society

Chorleywood: Elegance amongst the beeches

Early in the 1900s the famous architect Charles Voysey built a house for himself high above Chorleywood. It was a house in which 'all must be plain and practical. The sloping buttress walls to counteract the outward thrust of the heavy slate roof. The stepped tiles below the chimney pots are there to throw off the driving English rain'.

Voysey set the style for many elegant Chiltern houses amid the beeches. He was also one of the first commuters to Baker Street (where he had his practice).

'And wood smoke mingled with the sulphur fumes

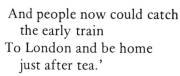

And people now could catch the early train
To London and be home just after tea.'

Sir John Betjeman

The Cedars Estate was developed between Rickmansworth and Chorleywood from about 1921 onwards. 'The estate will be laid out to provide village greens and open spaces with unusual stretches of wide and well-made roads. A portion of the beautiful woods will be left in their natural state.' There were prices to suit everyone on the Metropolitan estate amid the beech trees. From distinctive residences at £3250 to charming little brick built houses at £725. And a season ticket (3rd class) to Baker Street cost just £1 11s 3d a week.

Chalfont and Latimer: Mixed goods

Although in the 1930s the Metropolitan was mainly a passenger carrying railway, it did operate a number of freight trains. In 1932 it carried 1,015,501 tons of merchandise, plus 662,764 tons of coal, whilst minerals amounted to 2,478,212 tons, and livestock to 25,216 tons.

The locomotive is one of the 'K' class — the final type built for the Metropolitan Railway. The class had a curious ancestry. Just after the First World War ended, the Government ordered some locomotives based on South Eastern Railway design so that the workers at the Woolwich Arsenal could be kept employed. Only a few of the engines were built and the rest of the parts were then stored until disposed of. The Metropolitan's Chief Mechanical Engineer George Hally obtained the parts, designed the powerful 'K' class, had additional parts made and the locomotives entered service in 1924, being built by Armstrong Whitworth and Co. After 1937 they were sold to the LNER (together with all the larger Met steam engines) and were gradually withdrawn between 1943 and 1948.

Locomotive Club of Great Britain

**CEDARS ESTATE
RICKMANSWORTH
HERTFORDSHIRE**

Old Chalfont St Peter
The village centre about 1906.
Edwardian country walkers, after leaving the Metropolitan train at Chorleywood, would have strolled down to the valley and passed over the footbridge, whilst the villagers stared silently. The river Misbourne is left to be forded by farm wagons, for even outside the 'Greyhound' there is no sign of a motor car.

Buckinghamshire County Museum

Chalfont and Latimer: Right away to Amersham
The last passengers have run down the subway under the platforms to get the branch line train to Chesham. The guard of the Aylesbury train has waved his flag and we're about to pull out on the way to Amersham, the next stop. The spick-and-span engine is one of the 'H' class (No. 116) and the front carriage is one of the first batch of 'Dreadnought' carriages built in 1905.

A. W. Croughton Collection

Chesham: High Street 1900
A prosperous and busy town already well known for its local products — brushes, chairs and timber wares, as well as for its watercress. Special trains rushed the watercress to the London markets in the early days of Metro-land.

Buckinghamshire County Museum

Chalfont and Latimer: Change here for Chesham
This picture shows the station on 5 June 1933. The Chesham train waits behind one of the old 'E' class engines for the arrival of the main line train from London. On the far right a garage and car showroom is under onstruction to serve the needs of the growing community of London businessmen who have settled in the district.

A. W. Croughton Collection

Chalfont and Latimer: The 10.04 departure from Chesham
One hazy early June day in 1933, not many weeks before the Metropolitan Railway became part of the new London Transport. Kerr Stuart 'H' Class Locomotive, No. 108 designed by Charles Jones and introduced in 1920, pulls out of Chalfont station.

The ladies pull down the blinds in the First Class and flick over the pages of *Vogue* or *The Lady.* Retired businessmen contemplate a day on the golf course at Moor Park or a trip to town to visit their clubs and old acquaintances whilst they look at the latest events from Germany in *The Morning Post.* But nobody really cares. It's summer and the wayside banks are full of flowers.

A. W. Croughton Collection

Chesham
Steaming down the line past Quill Farm Wood to Chesham in the early 1930s is old 'E' class engine No. 78. She was built at Neasden in 1898.

Len's of Sutton

Chalfont and Latimer: The Old Berkeley Hunt
An early service advertised by the Metropolitan was the conveyance of horses from Finchley Road to the Chilterns. You could enjoy a day's hunting with the locals and be back in London for dinner. Here, the Old Berkeley meets for the opening hunt of the season on the terrace at Latimer House and even the maids up in the bedrooms have stopped their bed making and dusting to see the start.

Buckinghamshire County Museum

Chalfont and Latimer: How did it go?
Another meeting of the Old Berkeley, as spectators question the huntsmen on the success of their morning's sport. The time is about 1934.

Buckinghamshire County Museum

Chesham: Lord's Mill 1899
One of the few Chiltern mills that
have survived to the present day,
although the lane on the left is now
a busy road leading to Latimer and
Chenies. The great undershot wheel
was removed in 1900, but the mill
continued to use steam power and
was active until well after the
Second World War.

Authors' Collection

Chesham: Saturday afternoon rest
Between the Wars, Saturday mornings at least twice a month were spent at the office. But if you worked in the City or West End, you could make the most of the day. You could wear a sports jacket (with a chequered tie) and catch the Saturday lunchtime Pullman home to Chalfont or Chesham, and have a bite to eat and a drink on the way.

Now the lunch hour is over and the Pullman train has been divided in the Chesham yard. 'H' class locomotive prepares to run round the three 'Dreadnought' carriages in the platform (which is off to the right) whilst the Pullman car and the other two carriages wait in the yard until Sunday morning, when they will be run back to Neasden empty for cleaning.

A. W. Croughton Collection

Chesham: Drying out
A summer cloudburst in the Chess Valley, about 1920. Flood water had swept through the low-lying cottages, forcing the occupants to bring out their possessions — a sewing machine, mangle and an assortment of chairs whilst drying out operations were put in hand.

Authors' Collection

Chesham: Local bus
The Metropolitan contracted with a
number of local operators to run
horse-drawn buses to the depths of
the Metro-land countryside. This
bus is jogging along from Chesham
Station over the hills to Berk-
hamsted about 1880.
Buckinghamshire County Museum

Amersham: Off to London

The Chilterns were sprinkled by great beechwoods in which individual craftsmen, known as bodgers, worked away amongst the fresh timber on improvised lathes, turning out a vast assortment of wooden products. Their work would be collected, and perhaps assembled finally in the village before being taken to the London markets — often by Metropolitan goods train.

The vast pile of chairs in this picture is being taken by an appropriately named Mr Sawyer from Winchmore Hill near Amersham in September 1910.

Buckinghamshire County Museum

Amersham: Coach tour

A char-a-banc party on a Chiltern tour arrives at Old Amersham in the 1920s. An interesting photograph because it shows the group of old cottages which were demolished for road widening at the end of the 1930s. Note the early petrol pump outside what is now the Trust House hotel.

London Transport

Frith Hill, Great Missenden at the turn of the century. Two ladies, perhaps arrivals by Metropolitan Railway, pose on a very nasty road bend above the town. This hill was extremely popular with photographers at the time.

FRITH HILL, GT. MISSENDEN.

Last Day of Steam — No. 42070, a Fairburn-designed 2-6-4 tank locomotive, heads a special train entering Amersham station on 9 September 1961. Passenger steam services to Aylesbury ceased after this date.

This locomotive had a short life; it was built at Brighton in 1950 and was withdrawn in 1965.

Far from the Madding Crowd
The rural image of Metro-land, seen here at Looseley Row, west of Great Missenden. The countryman faced long hours of very hard work, and the head horseman was the highest paid farm worker at a time of low wages, before the appearance of the tractor in the mid-1930s.

Authors' Collection

Great Missenden: Chiltern Farming
A scene on a Chilterns farm in 1911. It is almost certainly late August and the weeks of heavy toil out in the fields are over. An early flail reaper stands on the right and the head horseman leads away his charges in the early evening sun, while behind him farm workers hurry to complete the stacks as threshing goes on at the far side. Visitors coming down from London on the Met and walking to a farm-yard like this were in a completely different world.

Buckinghamshire County Museum

Great Missenden: Rural by-ways
A picture from the Metropolitan Railway Guide of 1904. The lane is empty of traffic and the wide-wheeled cart has plenty of time to trundle up the hill, as it is not very likely that a motor-car will appear.

Authors' Collection

Wendover: Never Mind the Traffic
There's plenty of time to stand in the road and watch the man with the heavy plate camera get under his black cloth. It is very unlikely that one of those noisy, new fangled motor cars will come round the corner. This was the scene that greeted the visitor when he came up from the station and turned left into the High Street. The old cottages are still there, but the road has been widened and there's plenty of traffic.

Authors' Collection

"THE MET"

EXCURSIONS
To WENDOVER
(For the Military Camp)
and WEEK=END
TICKETS
TO
HERTFORDSHIRE and BUCKINGHAMSHIRE
From LONDON

MARCH, 1915,
and until further notice.

R. H. SELBIE,
Baker Street Station, N.W.   General Manager.
MARCH, 1915.

Wendover: Cheap trips to the camp
The *Railway Magazine* in the
autumn of 1914 reported a remark-
able scene at Wendover: 'At a short
distance from the railway station,
the great slopes are covered by
interminable stretches of wooden
trellis and skeletons of wooden-
framed houses. Some 20,000 troops
are now in training.'

The Metropolitan Railway was
always prepared to cash in on any
traffic and so it advertised
Excursions for 'all those desirous of
witnessing the making of an army'.

A long branch serving Halton
Camp at Wendover, was constructed in 1917 by German
Prisoners of War (they were also
put to work felling the local beech
woods). The branch was used to
take coal and freight to the camp,
which eventually became an RAF
Station. In recent years the branch
carried coal only. It was closed on
31 March 1963. The ten or twelve
wagon trains were always hauled
from the main line by Air Ministry
locomotives.

This interesting branch left the
main line on the east side of
Wendover Yard, protected by a
G.C. lower quadrant signal. Gates
over the Aylesbury Road were
worked by train crews. Its length
was 1¾ miles and the long passing
loop on this single line was out of
use some years before the branch
closed. At first trains were hauled
both ways, but later were hauled to
Halton and propelled to Wendover.

H. V. Borley

Wendover: Erection of the Boer War Monument

The stone obelisk on Coombe Hill, Wendover's monument to those local men who were killed in South Africa at the turn of the century, was unveiled on 4 November 1904. The monument stands on almost the highest point of the Chilterns — at a spot known to generations of walkers. There was a local subscription, and there was much pomp for the opening. The local band played 'See the Conquering Hero Comes' at the start of a procession up the hill from Wendover Clock Tower. We must expect that they were well-winded as they completed the steep ascent.

The monument was struck by lightning in 1938, reducing it to about the height shown in this picture. It was soon rebuilt, but has suffered a repetition of the event. The bronze plaque to the dead was looted in the early 1970s, and the list is now cut in stone.

Buckinghamshire County Museum

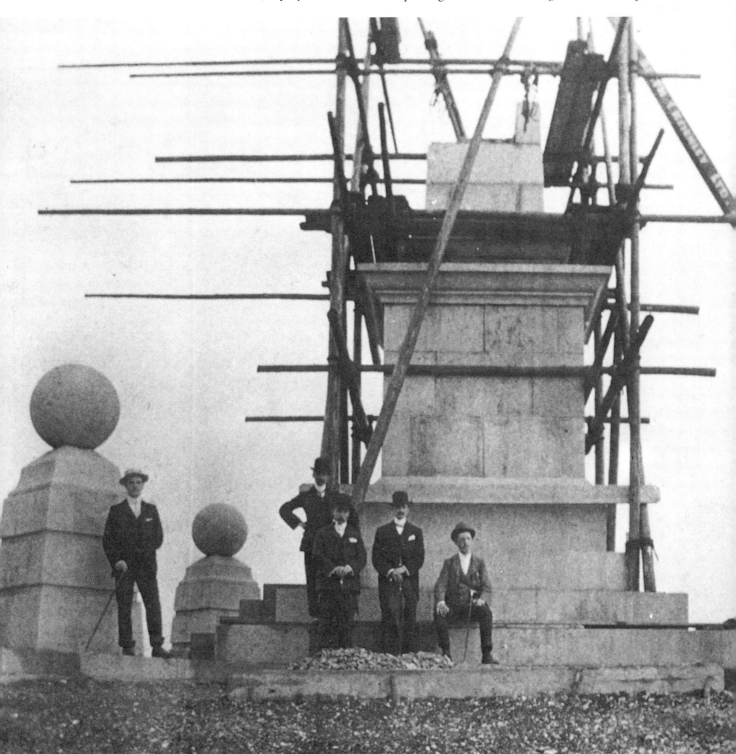

Aylesbury: Off duty

In later Metropolitan days two of the old Beyer-Peacock engines were kept for working the Brill branch from Quainton Road. Nos. 23 and 41 each ran a week's duty. No. 23 waits here at Aylesbury before returning to Neasden for a week's rest. But light engines waste company money, so a train of empty wagons is attached, which will probably be left at Neasden or Harrow yards. This locomotive worked until 1948 and is now preserved at the London Transport Museum at Covent Garden.

Authors' Collection

Wendover: The old windmill

A very rare photograph, dated 1903, showing the old tower mill when it was still worked by wind power. In the foreground is Wendover goods yard. Because houses gradually deprived the mill of wind power, the mill had to resort to mechanical assistance. The sails were removed in the 1930s.

Authors' Collection

Aylesbury: The original station
The young lady standing on the London platform at the old GWR station appears to know the engine man on the track very well. He is probably about to go to his locomotive which is possibly standing out of our picture to the right. The Aylesbury and Buckingham Railway had just become part of the Metropolitan Railway when this picture was taken by S. W. A. Newton, the Leicester man who photographed the Great Central Railway. The original GWR line from High Wycombe to Aylesbury had been broad gauge and if you examine the goods shed in the distance under the bridge, you can see the extra large archway built to accommodate the wider stock. The station at Aylesbury was rebuilt and enlarged when the Great Central opened and the new layout came into use on 1 January 1894. *Leicester Museums*

Aylesbury: Metropolitan express to the City in 1933
Just pulled in from Verney Junction, this train is in charge of one of the 'G' class engines built in 1915-16 by the Yorkshire Engine Company. With the exception of the first batch of 'A' class engines many years before, the four 'G' class locomotives were the only engines to bear names until the advent of the electric locomotives. This is No. 97 'Brill'. The others were: 94 'Lord Aberconway', 95 'Robert H. Selbie' and 96 'Charles Jones'.

H. Gael

Aylesbury
No.108, one of the 'H' class locomotives standing in the bay line at Aylesbury heading a train with milk van and 'Dreadnought' carriages on 17 April, 1933.

A. W. Croughton Collection

Aylesbury to Verney Junction & Brill

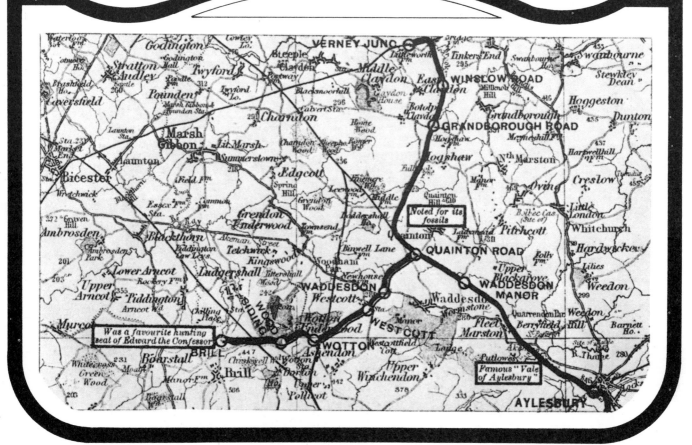

'The line is that which old George
Stephenson said was the right one
and was sure to be made one day.
Those were the old man's words to
me standing in Botolph Claydon,
and looking at the gap between
Quainton and Pitchcott.'

Letter from Sir Harry Verney
5 May 1890

Waddesdon: The Aviary Garden at Waddesdon Manor

One of the Rothschilds pauses in the 1890s amid the flowers of the aviary garden. Nearby is the site where building materials and fully-grown trees were transported to the summit of Lodge Hill, upon which the manor was constructed in the 1870s. The Wotton Tramway, as the Brill branch was then known, had been opened only a year or so previously and was used to bring the materials to the foot of the hill from a spur at Westcott Station. Telegraph wires had to be lowered to allow the extraordinary loads to be moved. Teams of Percheron mares from Normandy were employed to haul the loads from the terminus of the special branch. The gardens were designed by a Frenchman, M. Laine.

Buckinghamshire County Museum

Waddesdon: The village school
On 14 May 1890, some fifteen years before this photograph was taken, Queen Victoria had visited Waddesdon Manor, the great mansion created by Baron Ferdinand de Rothschild in the 1870s. The Queen was taken round the grounds in a bathchair drawn by a small pony, and an early movie film exists of the event.

King Edward VII, when Prince of Wales, came here by Metropolitan Railway, possibly travelling in the Rothschild Saloons, and he soon became a fairly frequent visitor. He alighted at Waddesdon Manor station, which the Met agreed to build for the Rothschild family. On the first visit the Prince's train was drawn by a locomotive decorated on each side tank with the Prince of Wales' feathers.

Waddesdon village, part of the estate, is well-built and tidy, like these little boys and girls in their cleanest Sunday-best clothes.

Buckinghamshire County Museum

Wotton Station 1933: School outing

A view taken near the end of the old railway's life. The station seems unusually busy with children — perhaps on a school outing from Aylesbury. The west side of the station was often occupied with cattle wagons.

Annie Kirby

Westcott
One of the Manning Wardle locomotives purchased in the 1890s for
work on the Brill branch. The track
is composed of flat-bottomed steel
rails laid down to replace the
original track in 1894. The building
in the centre is the booking hut —
one of the many buildings and
structures provided for the line by
the Oxford and Aylesbury Tramroad Company when it acquired
the line from the Wotton Tramway
company on the death of the Duke
of Buckingham. The building and
the house at Westcott are now the
surviving station structures.

Leicester Museums

Under Construction
View from the newly-constructed
bridge at Wotton (Met) station, at
the time of the building of the
Great Central spur line to Princes
Risborough in 1898. The Brill
branch line (far right) has been
newly ballasted following its
relaying in 1894. The station
buildings are also of that date.

Leicester Museums

Wotton: Relaying the track
This photograph was taken at the time of the construction of the Great Central Railway from Ashendon Junction to Calvert. At the time, four platelayers were employed on the Brill branch at 15 shillings (75p) a week. The foreman (named Varney and almost certainly the man in the foreground) received an extra 30p. When the Metropolitan took over the line, their wages were increased by 5p to bring their pay up to the level of other Met platelayers in the area.   *Leicester Museums*

Wotton: The other station

This station lay only 200 yards away from the rival Metropolitan one. The Great Central Railway between Calvert and the GWR at Ashendon Junction was built following a long argument between the two companies which reached a climax on 30 July 1898. The Met's Chairman, John Bell, had heard that his former office colleague William Pollitt (who had become General Manager of the GCR) proposed to run trains from the north of England on to the GWR line at Aylesbury, so by-passing the Met's main line south to Harrow, which was leased to the Great Central. Bell personally set the signals against this train. This event resulted in the Great Central concluding an agreement with the Great Western for a new joint route to London via Princes Risborough and High Wycombe.

In later years the rivalry was largely forgotten and the GCR stationmaster doubled for the Met station as well. Traffic tended to use the more direct GCR service to London rather than the Brill Line to Quainton Road. Here a carriage awaits the arrival of its owner on the Marylebone express from faraway London. The notice advertises the 'new suburban train service' which began on 2 April 1906 (March 1906 via Harrow). The GCR advertised its suburban services: 'Great Central Railway is the Line of Health.'

Annie Kirby

Wotton Underwood: The Kingswood branch

A loading note dated December 1888, requesting wagons to load with hay at Kingswood. This place, although shown as a station on some early maps, was served by the old horse tramway running from Wotton Underwood. It was never part of the Metropolitan's system, and was only leased by the earlier Oxford and Aylesbury Tramway from the Buckingham Estates.

Charles E. Lee

Wood Siding: Down leafy by-ways
It is hard to believe that this was part of the busy Metropolitan Railway — the same company that ran through the cuttings and tunnels beneath London and carried thousands daily to and from their work. But here at Wood Siding there are never any commuters, few day trippers, and few passengers at any time. Today this stretch of line has been completely covered in dense bushes and trees.

Authors' Collection

Wotton Estate Workers

In this remote part of Buckinghamshire, even the most devoted country walkers from London were seldom seen. The countryside remained one of the most peaceful in all the southern part of England. Aylesbury, the nearest town, would be unlikely to see those young estate workers (seen here dipping sheep in what seems to be an unnecessarily involved way) more than once a year. In those days, almost before 'wireless', they rose early for work (sometimes before 5am) and went to bed as soon as the light failed, for reading by oil-light was especially trying on the eyes.

Buckinghamshire County Museum

Wood Siding: In the depths of the woods
Beyer Peacock locomotive No. 23, far from its old haunts on the Inner Circle, passes slowly over the lane to Kingswood at Wood Siding. This halt was situated by the bridge which carried the Brill line over the GWR line to Bicester.

H. C. Casserley

Wood Siding: Thame Lodge
The line passing the pedestrian crossing at Thame Lodge. The lodge still stands on the lane up to Wotton Underwood. Trains had to run past here at 4mph.

F. H. Stingemore

Wotton Underwood: Tracing a vanished railway

At Wotton Underwood one of the authors pauses to check with two colleagues the contour variations. Very little is known of the Kingswood Branch, laid during the early years and abandoned before the first World War. As early as 1910, the *Railway Magazine* query column said nothing was known of the line. It was always an agricultural track, horse-hauled. By using the footpath from Wotton to reach a point where the hedge had altered (and by old maps) the old trackway, just under 1½ miles in length, could be traced. The Kingswood terminus, close to an old Tile works, was clearly not sited (as an old story suggested) by the Duke of Buckingham flinging his hat in the air! *Authors' Collection*

Church Siding: End of the Line

The end of the horse drawn section of line that served Church Siding, Wotton Underwood. The 'scotches' fixed to the conventional track are to stop trucks rolling on — and into the mud! The short section of rail nearest the camera is laid on longitudinal timbers — the original track of the 'Brill' system. This pictures dates from 1 December 1935, the day after the 'main' line had closed. By then the siding had been out of use for some considerable time.

F. H. Stingemore

Wotton Water Tower

The small branch line up to Church Siding, Wotton Underwood, branched off on the left of this picture. Trucks were hauled along the branch which once ran as far as Kingswood. Extra water facilities were required after the drought of the early 1880s, when local farm ponds had evaporated.

London Transport

Brill: Early Motive Power

Manning Wardle locomotive 'Brill No. 1', She was bought for £1000 and cost an extra £40 because Board of Trade regulations required a governor to be fitted to restrict the speed. She was named 'Earl Temple' after the chairman of the Oxford and Aylesbury Tramway. He actually owned the locomotive and rented it to the company at £2 a week. The engine arrived on the line in 1894. One of the men in this picture is almost certainly Driver H. Cross and he earned 30/- a week. Another man is probably W. Stevens, the fitter. After the line was leased to the Metropolitan Railway, Brill No. 1 — 'Earl Temple' — was re-named. The engine was sold to a contractor, Frank Hayes of London and was eventually used on the construction of the Great West Road!

Annie Kirby

Brill: Branch line train
Metropolitan Railway carriage 232,
believed to be a composite, with
milk van, cattle wagon and brake
van. The hills in the distance are
those through which the planned
westward extension of the branch
to Oxford would have passed.

Michael Crosby

Shunting at Brill Station, 1898
'Huddersfield', at 0-6-0 Class 'K'
Manning-Wardle locomotive built in
1876 and bought in 1878. It cost
£450, but the Company had
difficulty in paying. Earl Temple,
to whom the Tramway interests
were translated upon the death of
his uncle, the Duke of Buckingham
in 1889, purchased the locomotive
outright for the Company. It is seen
here shunting at Brill four years
later. Notice the indifferent state of
the track.

Annie Kirby

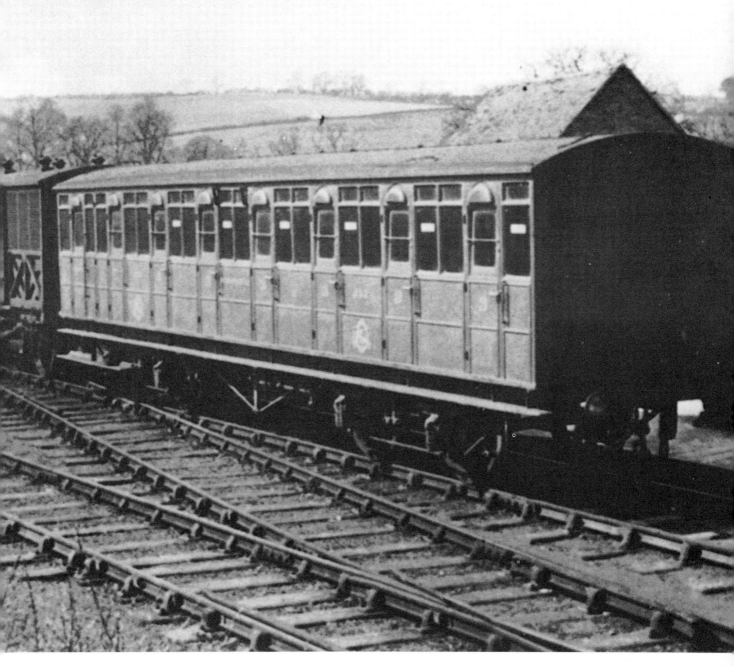

Brill

A young adventurer from London who has, at last, reached the remote terminus of the Metropolitan Railway at the foot of Brill Hill, just a few miles from Oxford, where once it was planned to extend the line. This picture shows how the platform height was raised when the Metropolitan carriages were introduced.

A. J. Hearn

Brill Station: Family gathering
The station staff and family, as well as the guard and brakesman pose by the ticket office c 1897. The locomotive on the right is one of the Manning-Wardle engines.
Annie Kirby

Locomotive No. 46 at Brill
It is seldom realised that other Metropolitan locomotives appeared at Brill apart from Nos. 41 and 23, the allocated locomotives for the line. One engine was in steam at any one time on a rota system. Every Monday the engine due for maintenance at Neasden would usually be worked up to Verney Junction and set off for London with loaded wagons. The relief engine worked light from Neasden to take over as duty locomotive.

When it was necessary to give major overhauls, other locomotives appeared — this is a very rare glimpse of such an event. The condensing gear, it will be noted, is missing from No. 46.

Michael Crosby

Brill Station Yard c1926
Here Driver Turner, who lived in the station cottage, had all the time in the world to pose with his pretty young daughter Grace and his guard (complete with whistle and pocket watch in waistcoat). School days for the elder children usually meant trips by train to Aylesbury or Princes Risborough, but this was a small price to pay for life in this land of flowers. This driver had started his driving career in the smoked filled caverns of the Inner Circle.

Authors' Collection

Waddesdon Road: In the country
An adventurous young man of the 1930s, with plus-fours and stick, stands at Waddesdon Road Station after leaving the Brill branch train. The remoteness is emphasised by the wooden platform, the ancient oil lamp, and the corrugated roofed station building.

A. J. Hearn

Brill: The old windmill

Brill, a small town perched high on a hill overlooking the Vale of Aylesbury, had at one time two windmills. This old print shows the now vanished mill. The surviving windmill's predecessor was erected about 1680 but was blown down. In 1757 there is an entry in the local records: 'expenses of rebuilding a Mill blown down at Brill, exclusive of old materials, and now lett [sic] to John Dilkins £175 5s.' Brill's mill always featured in Metro-land literature, as well as nearby Dorton Spa, a ghost spa of the Victorian age.

Buckinghamshire County Museum

Brill engine shed and water tower

The condensing pipe over the cylinder of Locomotive No.23 can be seen clearly on this unusual photograph which gives a view of the locomotive shed from the end of the platform ramp.

Michael Crosby

Quainton Road: Tea break

The building of the Great Central Railway across the green south Midlands to London was an important event — the last main line railway to be made in Britain. The Manchester, Sheffield & Lincolnshire Railway's Bill received Royal Assent in 1893 and work began on the 92 miles of new line from Nottingham to Quainton Road. The first coal train ran through to Marylebone on 25 July 1898 and the first passenger trains began on 15 March 1899.

The contractor for the construction work south to Quainton Road was Walter Scott and Co. It was the end of the 'navvy' age, too. In fact, on this last great construction job they had the help of mechanical aids. This picture shows a party of navvies taking a tea break during the construction of the new line just north of Quainton Road. The Metropolitan line to Verney runs over to the left. The photographer was S. W. A. Newton of Leicester. He made a complete and now unique record of the building of the line, as well as some pictures of existing railways adjacent or crossed by the new line.

Leicester Museums

Vale of Aylesbury: Off to the Harvest

Wagons loaded with estate workers cross a railway bridge on the way to the fields: a scene in the Metro-land of the 1920s in the Vale of Aylesbury. The labour force, before the age of tractors, was very large, and boys were expected to join as soon as they left school at 13 or 14 years. The cut corn was stacked in sheaves to dry in the field, and to await collection. Threshing machines pulled by steam tractors were a common, if noisy, sight as they trundled from farm to farm on contract.

Buckinghamshire County Museum

Hogshaw Bank

Beyond Quainton Road the Met line swept northwards towards Verney Junction, climbing the steep gradient to Grandborough Road. Along this track, photographed on the last day of the full passenger service, 4 July 1936, thundered the Met's Pullman Car trains. During the Second World War, the line was quite heavily used by goods trains moving cattle as well as war materials.

Authors' Collection

Winslow Road
The station seen from the nearby lane in the early 1930s. Here, almost fifty miles from Baker Street, life went on at a leisurely pace; each passenger would be known personally to the staff and there was plenty of time before the next train — often an hour or two.
London Transport

Winslow Road
Seen here in July 1936, at the end of passenger working. An LNER 'push-pull' train (which could be controlled from the rear end) prepares to leave the deserted platform.

Authors' Collection

Quainton Village
An ancient villager plods along the village road at Quainton, the nearest village to Quainton Road Station, the junction for the Brill Branch and the line to Verney Junction. Life here was hardly affected by the hope that Quainton Road would one day become, in Sir John Betjeman's words 'the Clapham Junction of the Met'. The windmill has now lost its sails, but the scene has changed little since the day this picture was taken on 15 April 1910.

Buckinghamshire County Museum

Granborough Road
The station as it was in April 1936.
Note the typical lattice-style Metro-
politan Railway footbridge —
examples still exist at Ruislip,
Wendover and Amersham.

Authors' Collection

Verney Junction
Metropolitan locomotive No. 109
('H' class of 1920) with a train of
three 'Dreadnought' carriages at
speed between Winslow Road and
Verney Junction on 4 July 1936, at
the end of its long journey from
Baker Street and the City.

F. H. Stingemore

Verney Junction
The old down outer home signal at
the approach to the junction. An
early Metropolitan Railway design.

F. H. Stingemore

Verney Junction: From the driver's cab

The signal is down for the final approach to the Met platform at Verney Junction. On the far side, in this July 1936 picture, a connecting train waits to take passengers towards Bicester and Oxford.

F. H. Stingemore

Verney Junction: End of the line

At Verney Junction, looking south in 1934. Trains are expected on both sides of the island platform.

Oil lighting was common at country stations; it gave a soft yellow light with less illumination than incandescent gas. Wicks needed constant trimming and attention, and many stations had an oil room, where tail lamps for the trains and guards' signal lamps could be refilled. In 1909 it was noted that Rickmansworth, Pinner, Chesham, Wendover and Aylesbury were lit by gas. Other stations used oil; Northwood went from oil to electricity in 1906, and Chorleywood and Amersham Stations changed to gas in 1912. Many Metropolitan stations on the Inner Circle Line were lit by gas until about 1912.

A. J. Hearn

to Buckingham

VERNEY JUNCTION

to Bletchley

to Leicester

Winslow Road

Grandborough Road

Grendon Underwood Junc

to O

QUAINTON ROAD

Waddesdon Manor

High St

L.M.S.

Waddesdon Road

Westcott

AYLESBURY

CHESH

Gasworks siding

Stoke Mandeville

Kingswood 'branch'

Wendover

Brill & Luggershall

Wotton

Great Missenden

Wotton

AMERSHAM

Chalfont & Latimer

Wood Siding

Chorley Wo

BRILL

Brickworks siding

Ashendon Junction

Princes Risborough

High Wycombe

THE OXFORD & AYLESBURY TRAMROAD COMPANY